Library Mania

Games & Activities for Your Library

by Charlene C. Cali

UpstartBooks

Janesville, Wisconsin

To my two daughters, Crista and Cassidee, for making my life complete.
You are my joy and inspiration.

Published by UpstartBooks
401 South Wright Road
Janesville, Wisconsin 53547
1-800-448-4887

Copyright © 2009 by Charlene C. Cali
Cover design: Debra Neu

The paper used in this publication meets the minimum requirements of American National Standard for Information Science — Permanence of Paper for Printed Library Material. ANSI/NISO Z39.48-1992.

Table of Contents

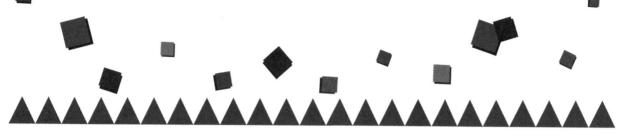

Introduction

Library Mania is designed to blend learning with fun and excitement in the media center. This curriculum is packed with ideas, games, activities, and lessons for teaching important library skills and is easy to use for the busy librarian. The lessons were developed over a five-year period by a practicing school librarian looking for ways to encourage students to enjoy and learn important library information skills. All lessons in this book are sequential and written with specific grade levels in mind. They also provide activities and opportunities for students to immediately practice the skills they are learning. Each lesson includes a library skills objective, a materials list, pre-lesson preparation directions, and a detailed lesson procedure. Several lessons also include extension activities, which the librarian may modify according to time available and student ability.

In the Library There Are Books

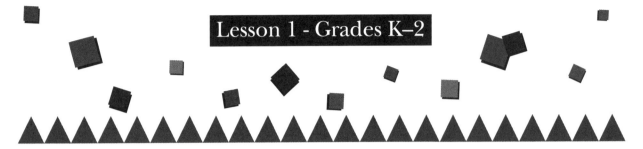

Lesson 1 - Grades K–2

Objective

Students will learn about what kinds of things are found in the media center.

Materials

In the Library There Are Books handout (page 8)

Pre-Lesson Preparation

Make a copy of the In the Library There Are Books handout for each student.

Lesson Procedure

1. Explain to students that they will be learning about what kinds of things can be found in the media center.

2. Take students on a tour of the media center. Be sure to point out different things that are found in the media center (e.g., books, computers, puppets, librarian, maps, puzzles, shelves, etc.).

3. Direct students to return to their seats. Teach students the following "In the Library There Are . . ." song, sung to the tune of "The Farmer in the Dell."

    In the library there are _____ (books).

    In the library there are _____ (books).

    All around you will see

    In the library there are _____ (books).

4. Direct students to choose another thing they see in the media center and replace the word "books" with their answer. Repeat several times.

5. Distribute the In the Library There Are Books handout. Assist students with folding the handout along the dotted line and then folding it accordion-style to make a booklet. If possible, make the booklets before the class arrives.

6. Depending on ability, direct students to draw or write one thing they see in the library on each page of their booklet. Share as time allows.

Extension

When the students return to the media center, begin the lesson by singing "In The Library There Are Books" with them. As they sing new verses about other things in the library, reinforce their mental maps of the media center by having them point in the direction where these other items can be found.

In the library
there are...

In the library
there are...

In the library
there are...

In the library
there are...

In the library
there are...

In the library
there are...

In the library
there are...

In the library
there are...

Meet the Book Care Buddies

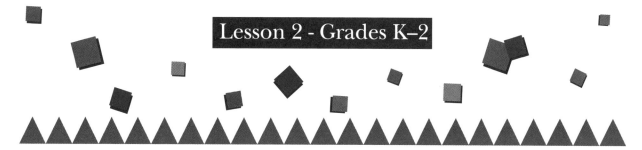

Lesson 2 - Grades K–2

Objective

Students will learn how to take proper care of their books.

Materials

- One copy of each Book Care Buddy (pages 10 – 14)
- Who is Taking Good Care of Their Books? handout (page 16)
- Copies of the I'm a Book Care Buddy Necklace (page 15)
- Yarn
- Crayons
- Hole punchers

Pre-Lesson Preparation

- Make copies of the Book Care Buddies; color and laminate.
- Make a copy of the I'm a Book Care Buddy necklace and Who is Taking Good Care of Their Books? handout for each student.
- Cut a long piece of yarn for each student's necklace.

Lesson Procedure

1. Explain to students that they will be learning about how to take care of their library books, and tell them that you have brought some friends to help them.

3. Introduce, read about, and discuss each Book Care Buddy.

4. Distribute an I'm A Book Care Buddy Necklace to each student. Direct students to draw a picture of themselves and color. Distribute yarn and hole punch necklace. Assist students with tying on their necklaces.

5. Display the Book Care Buddies in the media center as a reminder of the lesson.

Extension

Have students complete the Who is Taking Good Care of Their Books? handout.

Careful Carrie
Book Care Buddy

Careful Carrie always carries her books the right way. She hugs them when she walks to the media center and when she walks back to class. She doesn't want to drop or hurt them in any way, so she holds them tight. That's why she is a great Book Care Buddy!

Bookmark Ben
Book Care Buddy

Bookmark Ben remembers to use a bookmark to save his place when
he's reading. He knows that it will hurt the pages if he bends them
to mark his place. He reminds others to use a bookmark, too.
Thanks for being a great Book Care Buddy, Bookmark Ben!

Respectful Rita
Book Care Buddy

Respectful Rita turns the pages of the book very carefully. She reaches
for the top corner and turns the page slowly so that it doesn't rip.
She also tells the teacher when she notices that pages in a book have
been torn. Thanks for treating the books with respect, Rita!

Responsible Ralph
Book Care Buddy

Responsible Ralph remembers to wash his hands before looking at a book because he doesn't want to get the pages dirty. When he's finished with the book, he puts it in a safe place so that his younger sister won't color in it, and his dog won't chew on it. Thanks, Responsible Ralph!

Considerate Catie
Book Care Buddy

Considerate Catie remembers to bring her books back to the media center on time. She knows that another student might want to read them, too. She is a special Book Care Buddy to have!

I'm a Book Care Buddy Necklace

Draw a picture of yourself on the circle.

Cut out the circle.

Have someone help you punch holes for your yarn.

Tie the ends of the yarn through the holes.

Wear your necklace with pride!

I'm a Book Care Buddy!

Who is Taking Good Care of Their Books?

Color the pictures that show a good way to take care of your books.

ME

Looking Sharp in the Media Center

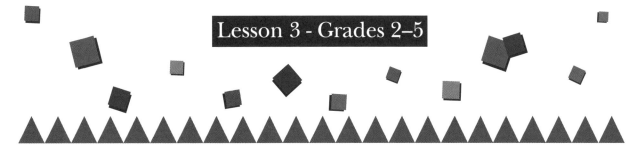

Lesson 3 - Grades 2–5

Objective

Students will learn about appropriate behavior in the media center.

Materials

- Silly clothes (e.g., crazy hat, big sunglasses, funny scarf, cape, grass skirt)
- A copy of How to Behave in the Media Center (page 19)

Pre-Lesson Preparation

- Put silly clothes in a large bag.
- Make a copy of How to Behave in the Media Center and cut into sentence strips.

Lesson Procedure

1. Explain to students that they will be learning about appropriate behaviors in the media center.

2. Tell students that when they are doing what they are supposed to do, they look "sharp" but, when they are not doing what they are supposed to do, they look a little "silly."

3. Choose a student who won't mind wearing silly clothes to demonstrate looking "sharp" or "silly." Have that student stand in front of the class.

4. Allow students to take turns choosing a sentence strip and reading an example of an appropriate or inappropriate behavior in the media center.

5. Each time an example is read, the class will decide if the action makes them look sharp or silly. If it makes them look silly, select a silly piece of clothing from the bag and put it on the chosen student. Repeat several times. Wearing the silly clothes enforces the point and offers a fun way to discuss expected behavior.

6. After the examples are read, tell the class that they have to help the student look "sharp" again. Each time a student gives an example of an appropriate behavior in the media center, have him or her remove a piece of the silly clothing from the chosen classmate. Repeat until all of the silly clothing is removed.

Extension

Make a bulletin board featuring Media Center Dos and Don'ts, and photos of students looking sharp or wearing silly clothes. You'll have students laughing all year long!

How to Behave in the Media Center

Appropriate Examples

You listened to instructions.

You walked in the media center.

You returned your books on time.

You followed directions.

You used your time wisely.

You were careful not to damage your books.

You shared materials.

You were ready to begin on time.

You put your book on the shelf correctly.

You waited quietly in line to check out your book.

You lined up quietly to go back to class.

Inappropriate Examples

You used your pencil as a bookmark.

You forgot to use a shelf marker.

You folded the page in your book to mark your place.

You leaned back in your chair.

You didn't clean your hands before reading a book.

You saw a book lying on the floor and didn't pick it up.

You forgot to raise your hand to ask a question.

You ran in the library.

You put a book back on the wrong shelf.

Things I Like to Do in the Media Center Bingo

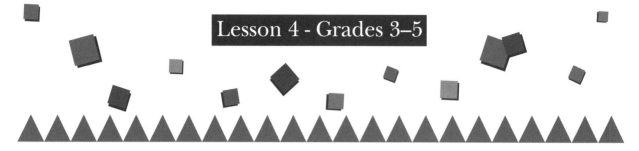

Lesson 4 - Grades 3–5

Objective

Students will learn things that their classmates like to do in the media center while sharing their own personal interests. This is a great activity to do at the beginning of the school year!

Materials

- Things I Like to Do in the Media Center Bingo worksheet (page 22)
- Who Is the Mystery Media Kid? reproducible (pages 23–24)

Pre-Lesson Preparation

- Make a copy of the Things I Like to Do in the Media Center Bingo worksheet for each student.

- Make enough copies of the Who Is the Mystery Media Kid? reproducible for each student to have a question. Cut the questions into strips.

Lesson Procedure

1. Explain to students that they will be learning about things that they and their classmates enjoy doing in the media center. Distribute the Things I Like To Do in the Media Center Bingo worksheet to each student.

2. Tell students that they are going to find out things that their classmates like to do in the media center and share things they like to do.

3. Direct students to walk around the media center with their Bingo worksheets and ask their classmates to sign a square on their worksheets that they enjoy doing.

4. A student "Bingos" when he or she has enough signatures either horizontally, vertically, or diagonally. Direct students to return to their seats after they "Bingo." Alternative option: Give students three to five minutes to get as many signatures as possible.

5. Tell students to circle three squares that list something that they will try this year in the media center. Discuss their answers.

6. Continue to explore students' favorite things to do in the media center by distributing a Who Is the Mystery Media Kid? question strip to each student. Direct them to answer the questions. Instruct students not to share their answers. Select five students to stand in front of the class. Collect their strips as they come forward. Choose one of the five to read aloud. Ask the class to guess which student wrote the answers. Allow four or five guesses, and then identify the Mystery Media Kid. Direct the student to return to his or her seat and select another student to participate. Continue as time allows.

Extension

Write on a poster board, "This year in the media center I would like to . . . " Lead a class discussion about activities that students would like to do in the media center (e.g., listen to read alouds, write poetry, learn how to use digital cameras, conduct group research, etc.).

Things I Like to Do in the Media Center Bingo

I like to read "Magic Tree House" books.	I like books about animals.	I like to do research.	I like to use computers.	I like to read books by Dr. Seuss.
I like books about the solar system.	I like to present my research.	I like to read books by Beverly Cleary.	I like to read the Boxcar Children series.	I like to do plays in the media center.
I like puppet shows.	I like to write stories.	I like to read biographies.	I like to read mysteries.	I like to read books that have true facts.
I like to read fairy tales.	I like to use PowerPoint presentations to share my information.	I like books that are made-up stories.	I like to search for information on the Internet.	I like to listen to stories read aloud.
I like to read poetry.	I like to use the dictionary.	I like to read books by Jan Brett.	I like to read autobiographies.	I like to check out books that teach me how to draw.

Who Is the Mystery Media Kid?

Who Is the Mystery Media Kid? Name _____

1. My favorite subject to read about is _____.

2. The title of my favorite book is _____.

3. My favorite book character is _____.

Who Is the Mystery Media Kid? Name _____

1. My favorite subject to read about is _____.

2. The title of my favorite book is _____.

3. My favorite book character is _____.

Who Is the Mystery Media Kid? Name _____

1. My favorite subject to read about is _____.

2. The title of my favorite book is _____.

3. My favorite book character is _____.

Who Is the Mystery Media Kid? Name _____

1. My favorite subject to read about is _____.

2. The title of my favorite book is _____.

3. My favorite book character is _____.

Who Is the Mystery Media Kid? Name _____

1. My favorite subject to read about is _____.

2. The title of my favorite book is _____.

3. My favorite book character is _____.

Who Is the Mystery Media Kid? Name _____

1. My favorite subject to read about is _____.

2. The title of my favorite book is _____.

3. My favorite book character is _____.

Who Is the Mystery Media Kid? Name _____

1. My favorite subject to read about is _____.

2. The title of my favorite book is _____.

3. My favorite book character is _____.

Who Is the Mystery Media Kid? Name _____

1. My favorite subject to read about is _____.

2. The title of my favorite book is _____.

3. My favorite book character is _____.

Who Is the Mystery Media Kid? Name _____

1. My favorite subject to read about is _____.

2. The title of my favorite book is _____.

3. My favorite book character is _____.

Who Is the Mystery Media Kid? Name _____

1. My favorite subject to read about is _____.

2. The title of my favorite book is _____.

3. My favorite book character is _____.

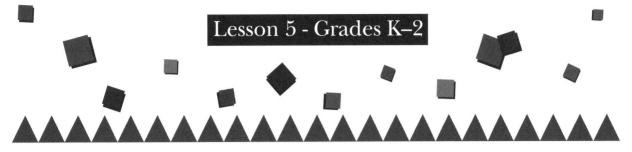

Sharp Shelves

Lesson 5 - Grades K–2

Objective

Students will learn how to place books properly on the shelves and how to keep the books in the correct order.

Materials

Sharp Shelves Shelf Marker (page 27)

Pre-Lesson Preparation

- Make a copy of the Sharp Shelves Shelf Marker on construction paper or card stock for each student. Note that you will have two shelf markers per page.

- Make a sample Sharp Shelves Shelf Marker.

- Place several books inappropriately on the shelves.

Lesson Procedure

1. Allow students to sit in close proximity to shelves of books.

2. Explain to students that it is important to help the books look sharp on the shelves. Further explain that the books look sharp when they stand up straight on the shelves with their spines pointing out. Point to where the spine of the book is and point to several books on the shelf that are placed correctly. Before class, position a few books inappropriately (e.g., flat on the shelves, left open on the shelves, turned backwards, lying on top of other books). Then ask students if they notice any books that are not looking sharp. Choose students to place the books on the shelves correctly.

3. Further explain that not only is it important for books to look sharp on the shelves, it is also important to keep them in order. Tell students that books have a "home" in the media center; a special spot on the shelves. Tell students that it is important to put the book back in its special spot after looking at it. Show students a copy of the Sharp Shelves Shelf Marker. Tell them that the shelf marker helps keep the books in the right spot. Demonstrate how to place the shelf marker in the book's place when the book is taken off the shelf. Then show students how to remove it when the book is placed back on the shelf. Choose several students to practice using the shelf marker.

4. Distribute a copy of the Sharp Shelves Shelf Marker to each student. Tell students to color the books that are looking "sharp" on the shelves.

5. Laminate the colored shelf markers and place them in a basket in the media center for students to use.

Sharp Shelves Shelf Markers

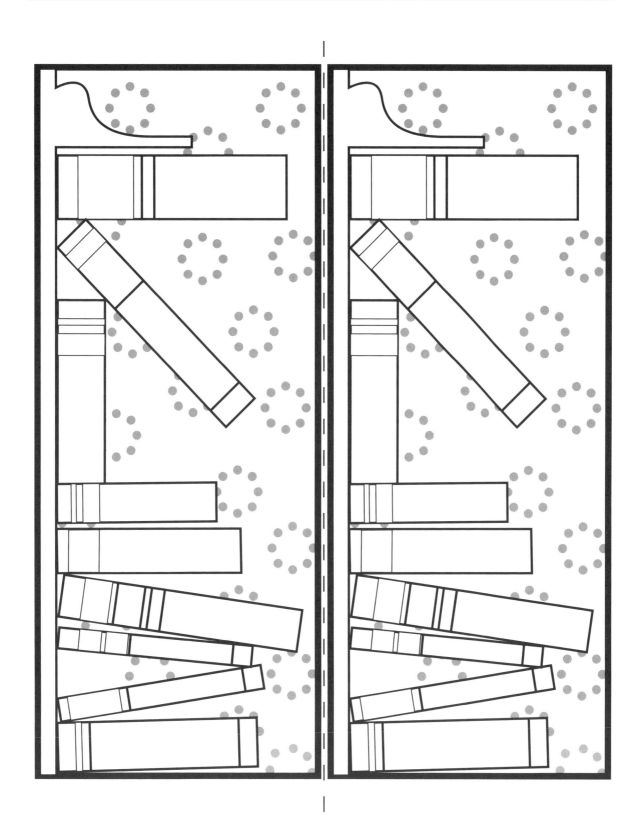

The Author Writes the Words for Us

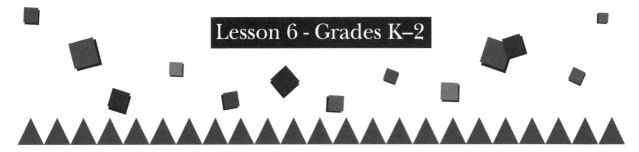

Lesson 6 - Grades K–2

Objective

Students will learn about the roles of the author and the illustrator in creating a book.

Materials

- Any picture book with the author and illustrator's names on the cover
- The Author and Illustrator handout (page 30)

Pre-Lesson Preparation

- Select a picture book that has the author and illustrator's names on the cover.
- Make a copy of The Author and Illustrator handout for each student.

Lesson Procedure

1. Tell students that they will learn what an author and illustrator do.

2. Explain that the author is the person who writes the words in a book. Choose a book and point to the author's name on the front cover, spine, and title page. Also, point to the words on the pages.

3. Explain that another important person who helped make the book is called an illustrator. Explain that the illustrator makes the pictures in the book. Point to the illustrator's name on the cover and point to the pictures.

4. Teach students the following song to help them remember how the author and illustrator help make

the book. Sing to the tune of "Mary Had a Little Lamb." Make the motion of writing when singing the author stanza. Make the motion of painting/drawing when singing the illustrator stanza.

> The author writes the words for us, words for us, words for us.
> The author writes the words for us,
> A diddle, a diddle, a dee.

> The illustrator makes the pictures for us, pictures for us, pictures for us.
> The illustrator makes the pictures for us,
> A diddle, a diddle, a dee.

5. Distribute copies of The Author and Illustrator handout. Tell students to color the pictures as a reminder of what the author and the illustrator do.

Extension

If time permits, have students color and cut out their author and illustrator pictures, sign their names to the back, and laminate for use as a bookmark. Periodically sing, "The Author Writes the Words for Us" song as a reminder of the author's and illustrator's jobs.

The Author and Illustrator

The author writes the
words for us,
words for us,
words for us.
The author writes
the words for us.
A diddle, a diddle,
a dee.

The illustrator makes
the pictures for us,
pictures for us,
pictures for us.
The illustrator makes
the pictures for us.
A diddle, a diddle,
a dee.

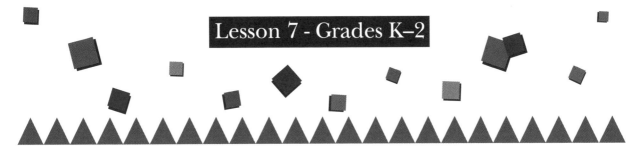

Let's Learn the Parts of a Book!

Lesson 7 - Grades K–2

Objective

Students will learn the parts of a book.

Materials

- Parts of a Book handout (page 33)

- Blank Parts of a Book handout (page 34)

- Crayons

Pre-Lesson Preparation

- Make a copy of the Parts of a Book handout and the blank Parts of a Book handout for each student in the class.

- Choose a picture book for the lesson.

Lesson Procedure

1. Explain to students that a book has many parts. Show them a picture book and explain the following parts while pointing to them on the book:

   Title: The title tells us the name of the book and helps us understand what the book is about.

   Author: The author writes the words. Explain that the word "by" is often in front of the author's name on the cover of the book.

   Illustrator: The illustrator creates the pictures. Explain that the words "illustrated by" are often in front of the illustrator's name on the cover of the book.

   Spine: The spine holds the pages together.

   Cover: The cover protects the pages.

   Publisher: The publisher prints the book. Explain that the publisher often has the words "publishing" or "press" with its name.

2. Teach students the following "Parts of a Book" song to help them remember the parts of a book. Sing to the tune of "Mary Had a Little Lamb."

The title tells the name to us, name to us, name to us.
The title tells the name to us,
A diddle, a diddle, a dee.

The author writes the words for us, words for us, words for us.
The author writes the words for us,
A diddle, a diddle, a dee.

The illustrator makes the pictures for us, pictures for us, pictures for us.
The illustrator makes the pictures for us,
A diddle, a diddle, a dee.

The spine holds the pages for us, pages for us, pages for us.
The spine holds the pages for us,
A diddle, a diddle, a dee.

The cover protects the pages for us, pages for us, pages for us.
The cover protects the pages for us,
A diddle, a diddle, a dee.

The publisher prints the book for us, book for us, book for us.
The publisher prints the book for us,
A diddle, a diddle, a dee.

3. Allow students to practice identifying the parts of a book. Distribute the Parts of a Book handout. Read the directions below one at a time. Tell students that they are going to practice their listening skills, too. Explain that you will only say each direction one time.

Directions

1. Circle the author's name with a blue crayon.

2. Put a star beside the illustrator's name with a purple crayon.

3. Underline the title with a red crayon.

4. Draw a square around the publisher's name with a green crayon.

5. Color the spine orange.

6. Color the cover yellow.

7. Write your name at the top of the page with a black crayon.

Extension

Pass out a picture book to each student. Call out the parts of a book and ask them to locate the parts on their individual books. Then, have students trade books and repeat. Do this several times. Distribute a copy of the blank Book Parts handout and direct students to select a picture book of their choice and fill in the blanks. Periodically throughout the year, sing the "Parts of a Book" song to review with students.

Parts of a Book

The Blue Bug

The Blue
Bug

Hall Press

The Blue
Bug

by
Tom Alden

Illustrated
by Pat Mann

Parts of a Book

Directions: Fill in the blanks.

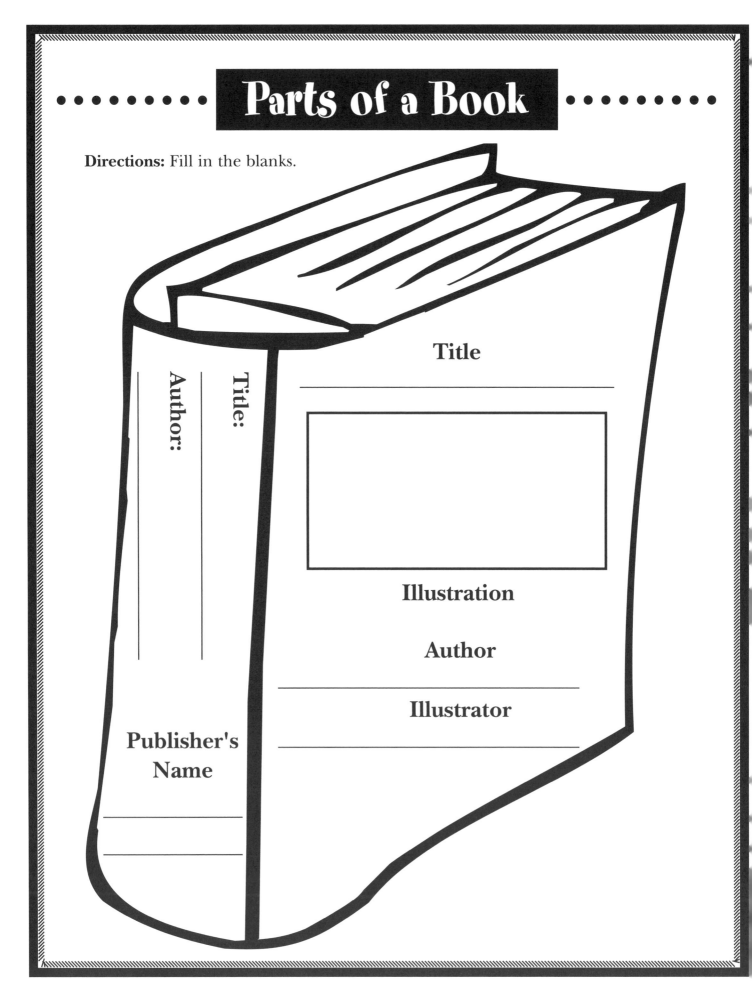

Title

Illustration

Author

Illustrator

Author:

Title:

Publisher's Name

Time-Out for Titles

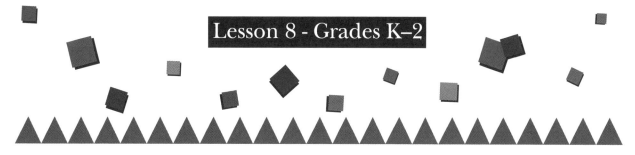

Objective

Students will learn that the title helps them find the correct book.

Materials

- Time-Out for Titles handout (page 36)
- Scissors for students

Pre-Lesson Preparation

- Make a copy of the Time-Out for Titles handout for each student.
- Choose a picture book for the lesson.

Lesson Procedure

1. Explain to students that the title tells us the name of the book and helps us to understand what the book is about.

2. Select a picture book and point to the title on the cover. Read the title and ask students what they think the book is about. Explain that the title often gives a clue about the book and is the first step to deciding if the book is one they are interested in reading.

3. Allow students to practice matching interests with titles. Distribute the Time-Out for Titles handout. Direct students to cut out the interests at the bottom of the page and place them on the correct title.

Time-Out for Titles

Cut the interests out at the bottom of the page.

Paste them on the correct title.

The Giving Hands	**Fun in the Sun**	**From Kittens to Cats**	**The Red Ball**
The Big Tree	**Growing a Flower**	**A Dog Named Blue**	**The Lonely Star**

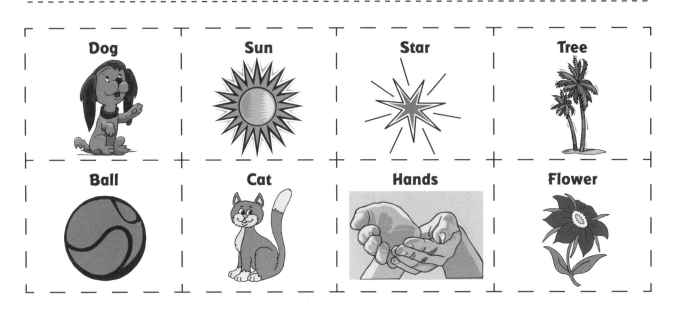

Dog   Sun   Star   Tree

Ball   Cat   Hands   Flower

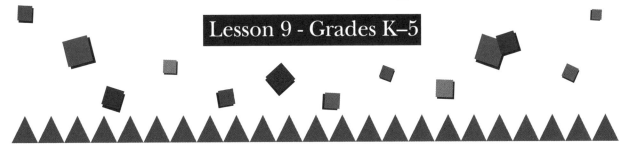

Places and Spaces

Lesson 9 - Grades K–5

Objective

Students will become oriented to the different places and spaces where books are found in the media center.

Materials

- Sections in the Library Signs (page 39)
- Five Index Cards
- Envelope

Pre-Lesson Preparation

- Make one copy of the Sections in the Library signs and laminate. Cut apart.
- Write the sections of the library on an index card. Write only one section per card. You may add other sections if you choose.

Lesson Procedure

1. Tell students that today, they will be learning about the different locations of books, materials, and resources in the media center.

2. Explain to students where the Fiction, Everybody, Nonfiction, Reference, and Magazine sections can be found in the media center. Give a brief description of what kinds of resources can be found in each section. Show them the Sections in the Library Signs as you explain.

3. Display the signs in their appropriate sections of the media center.

4. Place the index cards (with the sections written on them) in an envelope.

5. Have students practice learning where the different resource sections are in the media center by playing Places and Spaces. Direct students to choose a sign to stand by while you count to five. When you reach five, draw a section from the envelope. Students who chose to stand by that section must sit down at their seats. Put the section card back into the envelope, and repeat, asking students to move to a different section as you count to five. Continue with rounds until only one student is left standing. If you wish, present the final student with a reward (e.g., bookmark, sticker). Repeat as time allows.

Extension

Replace sections in the library with character names from a story or book titles by an author being studied. Have them stand by the character's name or by one of the books being studied. In addition, distribute a map of the library to older students and direct them to fill in the sections.

Sections in the Library Signs

Fiction

Nonfiction

Everybody

Reference

Magazines

Before or After: ABC Order

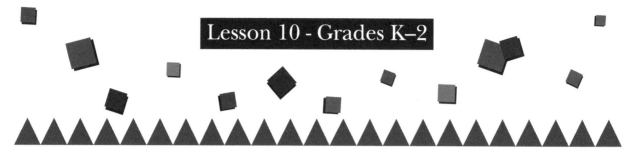

Lesson 10 - Grades K–2

Objective

Students will learn that books are arranged in alphabetical order.

Materials

- ABC Order Cards (pages 41 – 43)
- Books Are in ABC Order handout (page 44)

Pre-Lesson Preparation

- Make a copy of the ABC Order Cards and laminate.
- Make a copy of Books are in ABC Order handout for each student.

Lesson Procedure

1. Ask students where they see books in the media center. (Answer: They are mostly on the shelves.)

2. Tell students that books are put on the shelves in ABC order.

3. Practice ABC order by playing Before or After. Direct students to sit in a circle.

4. To play Before or After, first shuffle the ABC Order cards and place them face-down in rows of five in the middle of the circle so that all students can see. Choose a student to begin. Turn over the first card. Ask the student if he thinks that the next card will come before or after this card in the alphabet. When the student guesses, turn over the next card. If correct, the student gets to guess if the next card is before or after the current card in the alphabet. If incorrect, choose another student to guess. Continue until all cards have been turned over.

5. Distribute the Books Are in ABC Order handout. Direct students to cut out the books and place them in ABC order on the shelves.

Extension

After the activity, choose one student at a time to put the cards in order from A–Z. Sing the ABC song.

ABC Order Cards
(A–I)

A B C

D E F

G H I

ABC Order Cards
(J–R)

J K L

M N O

P Q R

ABC Order Cards (S–Z)

S T U

V W X

Y Z

Books Are in ABC Order

Cut out the books and place them in ABC order on the shelves.

_____

(Shelf)

_____

(Shelf)

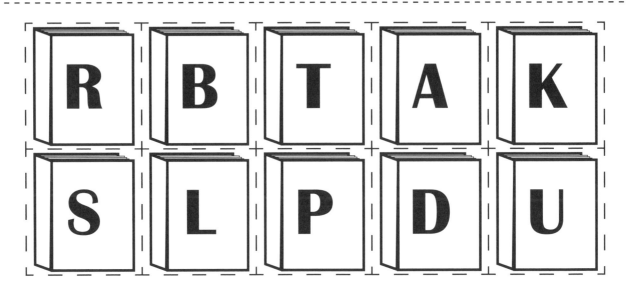

ABC Order by Author's Last Name

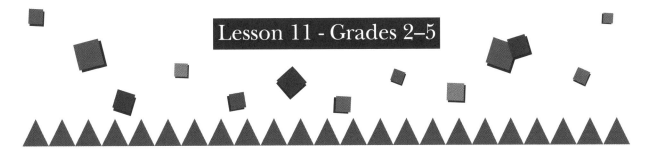

Lesson 11 - Grades 2–5

Objective

Students will learn to identify the author's name on the cover of a book and learn that fiction books are put in ABC order by using the first letter of the author's last name.

Materials

- ABC Order by Author's Last Name example (page 47)
- Several Copies of ABC Order by Author's Last Name Cards (page 49)
- Author ABC Order handout (page 48)
- Laminator
- Envelopes

Pre-Lesson Preparation

- Make a copy of the Author ABC Order handout for each student.
- Make one copy of the ABC Order by Author's Last Name example and laminate.
- Copy the ABC Order by Author's Last Name Cards so that each group of 3–4 students can have a complete set of cards (enlarge if desired).
- Laminate and cut the cards apart, and put them into envelopes (one set per envelope).

Lesson Procedure

1. Explain to students that fiction books, which are made-up stories, are put on the shelves in ABC order.

2. Review with students what the author does (writes the book). Explain that be-cause the author writes the book, we use the first letter of his or her last name to put the books in ABC order on the shelves.

3. Show students the ABC Order by Author's Last Name example, and point out where the author's name is on the cover of the book. Point to the first letter of the last name. Explain again that we use the first letter of the author's last name to put the books in ABC order.

4. Distribute the Author ABC Order handout. Direct students to write the authors' names in ABC order as they would be found on the shelves in the library.

5. Divide students into groups of three or four. Distribute a set of laminated ABC Order by Author's Last Name Cards to each group. Allow them to work together to put the books in ABC order using the first letter of the author's last name.

Extension

Have students stand up and put themselves in line alphabetically by last name. Then have them decide where you would belong in their line. When they correctly determine your place, pretend you have a different last name and ask them where you should stand now. Repeat as time permits.

The Happy Tree

by James **S**mith

Author
ABC Order

Dr. Seuss   1. _____

Jan Brett   2. _____

Mo Willems   3. _____

Eric Carle   4. _____

Bill Martin   5. _____

David Adler   6. _____

ABC Order by Author's Last Name Cards

A Star by Jan **H**owe	**Little Dog** by Don **A**llan	**A Quiet Parrot** by Sarah **M**ead	**A Rainy Day** by Justin **P**enn
Pig's Party by Pearl **O**wen	**The Funny Frog** by Chris **B**owen	**Janna's Birthday** by John **S**tewart	**The Big Ball** by Pam **C**hapman
The Snowman by Fred **R**edmond	**Happy Toes** by Tracy **D**illard	**The Talking Cat** by Paul **G**aston	**Mindy's Shoes** by Brenda **T**ate

Introducing . . . Call Numbers!

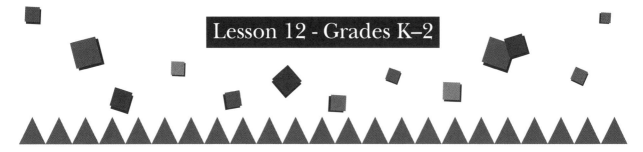

Lesson 12 - Grades K–2

Objective

Students will be introduced to call numbers and learn how they are used to put books in ABC order on the shelves.

NOTE: In this lesson, I refer to the "Everybody" section of the library. If this is not a term you use in your library, just replace my terminology with what works best for you and your students. The reproducibles in this lesson can easily be adapted to your library with a little white-out and a black marker, or serve as guides, should you wish to create your own.

Materials

- Introducing Call Numbers example (page 52)
- Author Call Number Match handout (page 53)
- Introducing Call Numbers Cards (page 54)
- Color the Correct Call Number handout (page 55)
- Shelve the Books! handout (page 56)
- A picture book
- Envelopes, scissors, and glue for students

Pre-Lesson Preparation

- Select a picture book for the lesson.
- Make one copy of the Introducing Call Numbers example.
- Make a copy of the Introducing Call Numbers Cards for each group of 3–4 students.
- Cut the cards apart and laminate. Keep sets separate using envelopes.
- Make enough copies of the Color the Correct Call Number and Shelve the Books! handouts for each student.
- Make enough copies of the Author Call Number Match handout for each student.

Lesson Procedure

1. Tell students that every book in the library has a home—a special place where it lives in the library—so library books need an address.

2. Explain to students that a book's address in the library is called its call number. Help the students remember what the call number is by singing "The Call Number Tells the Book's Address" to the tune of "Mary Had a Little Lamb."

   The call number tells the book's address, tells the book's address, tells the book's address.

   The call number tells the book's address,
   A diddle, a diddle, a dee.

3. Show students the Introducing Call Numbers example. Tell them that the book's address, or call number, can be found on the spine of the book. Point to the call number on the selected picture book.

4. Tell students that the first letter of the call number is an E, which tells us where the book's home is in the library. Explain that the E stands for the Everybody section.

5. Tell students that the second letter on the call number stands for the first letter of the author's last name.

6. (Grades 1–2) Distribute a copy of Author Call Number Match handout to each student. Direct students to match the author with the correct call number

7. Remind students that books are put on the shelves in ABC order by the author's last name.

8. Option 1: (Grades 1–2) Divide students into groups of three or four. Distribute a set of laminated Introducing Call Numbers Cards to each group. Allow them to work together to put the Call Numbers in ABC order as they would be found on the shelves.

   Option 2: (Grades 1–2) Give each student a copy of the Shelve the Books! handout and direct them to cut the books out and paste them in the correct order on the shelves.

   Option 3: (Grades K–2) Hide the laminated ABC Order cards from the "Before or After: ABC Order" lesson in the library. Direct students to find one of the cards and then find a book whose author's last name begins with the letter they found. Students may enjoy their book at their seat as long as time allows.

   Option 4: (Grades K–2) Distribute the Color the Correct Call Number handout and direct students to color in the animals holding the correct "address" for author Doreen Cronin.

Introducing . . .
Call Numbers!

The Turtle

by
Alice **S**mith

E
S

Author Call Number Match

Draw a line from each author to the correct call number.

1. Bill Peet

2. Eric Carle

3. Mo Willems

4. Jan Brett

5. Marjorie Sharmot

6. Leo Lionni

7. Tedd Arnold

8. Mem Fox

9. Jane Yolen

10. Lois Ehlert

E
S

E
E

E
P

E
A

E
C

E
W

E
B

E
Y

E
F

E
L

Introducing . . . Call Numbers Cards

A Star by Jan **H**owe **E** **H**	**Little Dog** by Don **A**llen **E** **A**	**A Quiet Parrot** by Sarah **M**ead **E** **M**	**A Rainy Day** by Justin **P**enn **E** **P**
Pig's Party by Pearl **O**wen **E** **O**	**The Funny Frog** by Chris **B**owen **E** **B**	**Janna's Birthday** by John **S**tewart **E** **S**	**The Big Ball** by Pam **C**hapman **E** **C**
The Snowman by Fred **R**edmond **E** **R**	**Happy Toes** by Tracy **D**illard **E** **D**	**The Talking Cat** by Paul **G**aston **E** **G**	**Mindy's Shoes** by Brenda **T**ate **E** **T**

Shelve the Books!

Help put the books back in the correct order on the library shelves!
Cut out each book and paste them in the correct order.

_____

(Shelf)

_____

(Shelf)

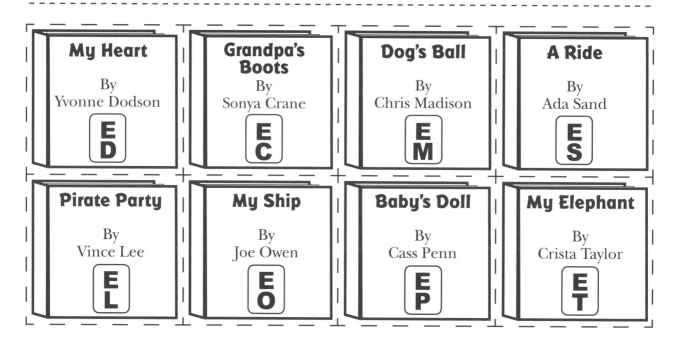

Let's Learn about Fiction Call Numbers

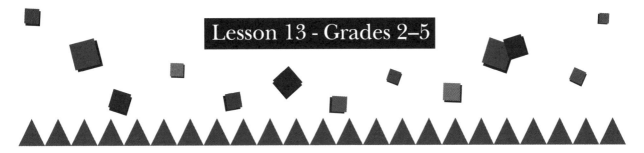

Lesson 13 - Grades 2–5

Objective

Students will learn about fiction call numbers and how they are organized on the shelves.

NOTE: In this lesson, I refer to the "Everybody" section of the library. If this is not a term you use in your library, just replace my terminology with what works best for you and your students. The reproducibles in this lesson can easily be adapted to your library with a little white-out and a black marker, or serve as guides, should you wish to create your own.

Materials

- Let's Learn about Fiction Call Numbers example (page 59)
- Write the Call Number handout (page 60)
- Putting Fiction Call Numbers in Order (page 61)
- Let's Learn about Fiction Call Numbers Cards (page 62)
- Shelve the Books! handout (page 63)

Pre-Lesson Preparation

- Make one copy of the Let's Learn about Fiction Call Numbers example.
- Make one copy of the Let's Learn about Fiction Call Numbers Cards for each student.
- Make a copy of the Shelve the Books! handout for each student.
- Make one copy of the Write the Call Number handout for each student.
- Make a copy of the Putting the Fiction Call Numbers in Order for each student.

Lesson Procedure

1. Tell students that every book in the library has a home—a special place where it lives in the library, so it needs an address.

2. Explain to students that a book's address in the library is called its call number.

3. Show students the Let's Learn about Fiction Call Numbers example. Tell students that the book's address, or call number, can be found on the spine of the book.

4. Explain that the first part of the call number tells us which section the book can be found in the library. Explain that E stands for the Everybody section where picture books are found. Tell students that the second part of the call number is the first letter of the author's last name. Tell students that FIC stands for the Fiction section. Explain that the second part of the Fiction call number is the first three letters of the author's last name.

5. Explain to students that books are put on the shelves in ABC order by the author's last name.

6. Distribute a copy of the Write the Call Number handout to each student, and direct them to write down the correct call number for each book, and put the books in ABC order as they would appear on the shelves.

7. Distribute a copy of Putting the Fiction Call Numbers in Order handout to each student, and direct them to complete it.

8. Distribute a copy of the Let's Learn about Fiction Call Number Cards handout and a Shelve the Books! handout to each student. Direct students to cut out each book card, and paste them in the correct order on the Shelve the Books! handout.

Extension

- Choose one student at a time to draw a card from the Let's Learn about Fiction Call Numbers Cards, and put it in the correct place on the shelves in the Fiction section.

- Make an additional copy of the Let's Learn about Fiction Call Numbers Cards, cut apart, and laminate. Students can participate in a matching activity with the cards and then put them in ABC order as they would be found on the shelves.

Let's Learn about Fiction Call Numbers

My Cat	Wind Storm
by	by
Pat **S**ummers	Tim **Byr**d
E S	FIC BYR

Write the Call Number

Write the correct <u>Everybody</u> call number as it would appear on the spine label of a book. Then number the call numbers 1-5 on the lines in the correct order that they would be found on the shelves.

Example: Jan Brett

E
B

1. Ezra Jack Keats

_____

2. Doreen Cronin

_____

3. Leo Lionni

_____

4. Cynthia Rylant

_____

5. Dr. Seuss

_____

Write the correct <u>Fiction</u> call number as it would appear on the spine label of a book. Then number the call numbers 1-5 on the lines in the correct order that they would be found on the shelves.

Example: Beverly Cleary

FIC
CLE

1. James Marshall

_____

2. Phyllis Reynolds Naylor

_____

3. Scott O'Dell

_____

4. J.K. Rowling

_____

5. Jerry Spinelli

_____

Putting Fiction Call Numbers in Order

Look at the Everybody and Fiction call numbers in each example.
In each example, number the call numbers (1–8) as they would be found on the shelves.

Example 1

E J	E A	E S	E C	E F	E V	E R	E T
___	___	___	___	___	___	___	___

Example 2

FIC ARA	FIC AEO	FIC TEL	FIC NUN	FIC LEP	FIC REN	FIC BIH	FIC TRA
___	___	___	___	___	___	___	___

Example 3

FIC THR	FIC HOC	FIC RLA	FIC PEN	FIC MUR	FIC PAL	FIC CUB	FIC COP
___	___	___	___	___	___	___	___

Let's Learn about Fiction Call Numbers Cards

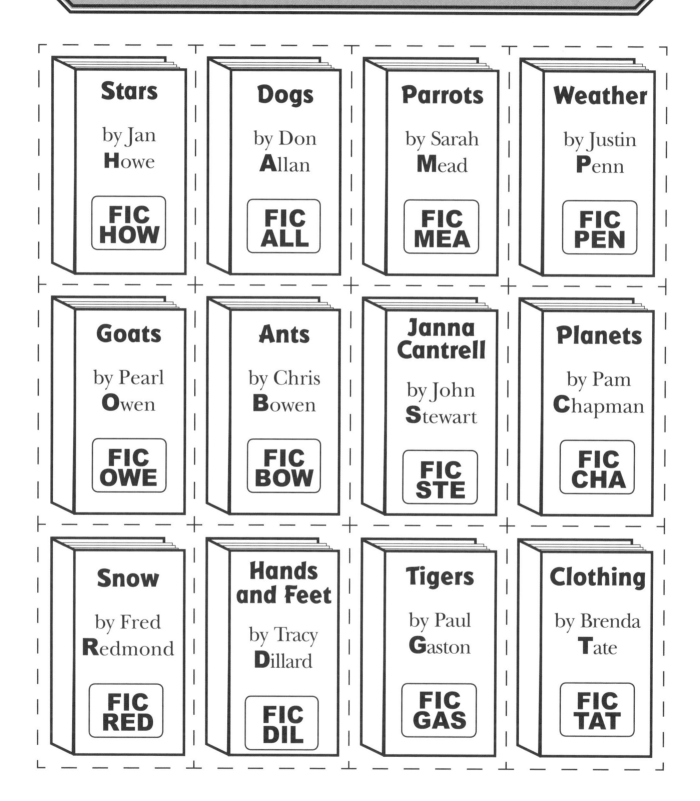

Stars

by Jan **H**owe

FIC
HOW

Dogs

by Don **A**llan

FIC
ALL

Parrots

by Sarah **M**ead

FIC
MEA

Weather

by Justin **P**enn

FIC
PEN

Goats

by Pearl **O**wen

FIC
OWE

Ants

by Chris **B**owen

FIC
BOW

Janna Cantrell

by John **S**tewart

FIC
STE

Planets

by Pam **C**hapman

FIC
CHA

Snow

by Fred **R**edmond

FIC
RED

Hands and Feet

by Tracy **D**illard

FIC
DIL

Tigers

by Paul **G**aston

FIC
GAS

Clothing

by Brenda **T**ate

FIC
TAT

Shelve the Books!

Cut out each of the books and put them in the correct order on the shelves.

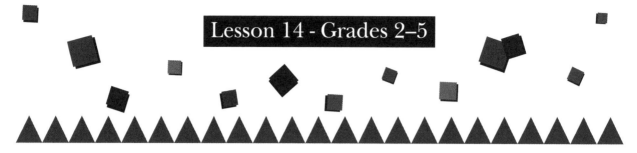

Fiction 7-UP

Lesson 14 - Grades 2–5

Objective

Students will practice putting fiction call numbers in the correct order.

Materials

- Fiction Call Numbers Cards handout (page 65–66))

Pre-Lesson Preparation

- Make one copy of each Fiction Call Numbers Cards handout; cut apart and laminate.

- To participate in this lesson, students must already understand how fiction call numbers are organized.

Lesson Procedure

Explain to students that they will be practicing putting fiction call numbers in the correct order by participating in Fiction 7-UP.

How to Play Fiction 7-UP:

- Distribute a Fiction Call Number Card to each student.

- Choose seven students to stand in the front of the class with their Fiction Call Numbers. Direct them to stand in the correct Fiction Call Number order. Direct the remaining students to put their heads down and hold up one thumb.

- The seven students will each choose one person by tapping his or her thumb.

- When a student is chosen, he or she will put his or her thumb down.

- The seven students should then stand in front of the class again in the correct Fiction Call Number order. When they are finished, ask the remaining students to raise their heads.

- The students who were chosen will try to guess which student chose them. Each student gets one guess only. If correct, the standing student sits down and is replaced by the one who guessed correctly. That student comes to stand in front of the class with his or her fiction call number and all seven students must stand in the correct order.

- Repeat as time allows.

Fiction Call Numbers Cards

FIC ABR	FIC BAR	FIC CHR	FIC DUN
FIC ECH	FIC FUL	FIC GIL	FIC HEP
FIC IEL	FIC JAS	FIC KET	FIC LAB
FIC MCD	FIC NOD	FIC AOT	FIC PRO

Fiction Call Number Cards

FIC RUE	FIC SLE	FIC TUL	FIC UHL
FIC VAN	FIC WYN	FIC YOD	FIC ZIM
FIC AEN	FIC CAL	FIC GAH	FIC HIL
FIC JEN	FIC SUW	FIC WES	FIC YEL

What Are Nonfiction Call Numbers?

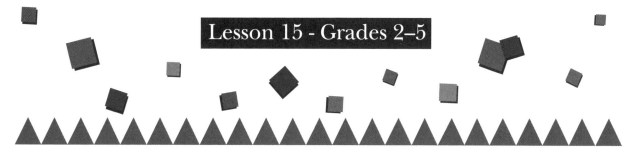

Lesson 15 - Grades 2–5

Objective

Students will learn how nonfiction call numbers are organized on the shelves.

Materials

- Learning about Nonfiction Call Numbers example sheet (page 69)
- Putting Nonfiction Call Numbers in Order handout (page 70)

Pre-Lesson Preparation

- Make one copy of the Learning About Nonfiction Call Numbers example.
- Make a copy of the Putting Nonfiction Call Numbers in Order handout for each student.

Lesson Procedure

1. Tell students that every book in the library has a home—a special place where it lives in the library—so every book needs an address.

2. Explain to students that a book's address in the library is known as the call number.

3. Show students the Learning about Nonfiction Call Numbers example on an overhead or document camera. Explain the following:

   a. The call number is found on the spine.

   b. Nonfiction call numbers are called Dewey Decimal call numbers.

   c. Nonfiction books (true books) have call numbers that are a combination of numbers and letters.

   d. The first part of the Dewey Decimal call number is made up of numbers. A nonfiction book can have a number ranging from 000 to 999. Some of the numbers may have a decimal point (.) in them.

e. When nonfiction books are put on the shelves, they are put in numerical order from the lowest Dewey Decimal call number to the highest Dewey Decimal call number.

f. The second part of the nonfiction call number is the first three letters of the author's last name.

g. Explain that if two or more books have the same Dewey Decimal call number, the books are placed in order alphabetically by the authors' last names.

4. As a class, put the books found on the Learning about Nonfiction Call Numbers example in the correct order.

5. Distribute the Putting Nonfiction Call Numbers in Order handout and direct students to complete.

Learning about Nonfiction Call Numbers

- The call number is found on the spine.

- Nonfiction call numbers are called Dewey Decimal call numbers.

- Nonfiction books (true books) have call numbers that are made up of numbers and letters.

- The first part of the Dewey Decimal call number is made up of numbers. A book can have a number from 000 to 999. Some of the numbers may have a decimal point (.) in them.

- When nonfiction books are put on the shelves, they are put in number order from the lowest Dewey Decimal call number to the highest Dewey Decimal call number.

- The second part of the Nonfiction call number is the first three letters of the author's last name.

- If two or more books have the same Dewey Decimal call number, the books are placed in order alphabetically by the authors' last names.

Example 1

811	225	400	400	721
BAR	RUN	PAR	ACK	CAL
___	___	___	___	___

Example 2

910	523	525	610.5	610.2
ABE	RAN	BAN	ROP	MAR
___	___	___	___	___

Putting Nonfiction Call Numbers in Order

Look at the nonfiction call numbers in each example. Number (1–8) the nonfiction call numbers in the order you would find them on the shelves.

Example 1

963 ABE	233 PER	600 BER	100 GUL	400 CAL	720 ZIN	625 DUN	811 PLU
_____	_____	_____	_____	_____	_____	_____	_____

Example 2

340 ARA	960 BUL	821 TIL	205.5 NUN	205.1 LEP	400 REN	551 PLA	910 TRA
_____	_____	_____	_____	_____	_____	_____	_____

Example 3

550 THR	550 HEN	733.1 RLA	735.2 PEN	225 SHI	180 PAL	645 CUB	300 COP
_____	_____	_____	_____	_____	_____	_____	_____

The Dewey Decimal Way

Lesson 16 - Grades 2–5

Objective

Students will learn about the Dewey Decimal system.

Materials

- Dewey Decimal System handout (page 72)

Pre-Lesson Preparation

- Make a copy of The Dewey Decimal System handout for each student.

Lesson Procedure

1. Explain to students that nonfiction books are organized by a method called the Dewey Decimal System. This system was named after its creator, Melvil Dewey, who said that nonfiction books should be grouped together according to their subjects. For example, all books about science should be put together, all books about people should be put together, all books about how to make things work should be put together, and so on.

2. Distribute The Dewey Decimal System handout and explain the ten different Dewey groups. If you have time, provide further examples of the classifications.

3. Direct students to practice matching subjects with the correct Dewey Decimal number group by completing the assignment at the bottom of The Dewey Decimal System handout.

4. Discuss the answers.

The Dewey Decimal System

000-099	**General Works**—Encyclopedias, atlases, newspapers, computers
100-199	**Philosophy**—Books about studying, thinking, and feeling
200-299	**Religion**—World religions, mythology
300-399	**Social Sciences**—Laws, governments, fairy tales, folktales, customs, transportation, holidays
400-499	**Languages**—Grammar, French, German, Spanish, etc.
500-599	**Science**—Rocks, animals, insects, mathematics, the solar system, weather, plants
600-699	**Technology (How Things Work)**—cooking, pet care, farming, medicine, inventions
700-799	**Arts and Recreation**—Painting, photography, arts and crafts, sports, music, riddles
800-899	**Literature**—Poems, plays, short stories
900-999	**History and Geography**—History, travel, geography, biography

Using the Dewey Decimal chart above, write the number group where you would find books about the following topics:

1. Animals _____

2. World War II _____

3. Limericks _____

4. Jupiter _____

5. Spanish _____

6. The Bible _____

7. Football _____

8. Honeybees _____

9. Cat Care _____

10. Cinderella _____

11. Helen Keller _____

12. Punctuation _____

13. New York _____

14. Encyclopedia _____

15. New Ideas _____

16. New Year's Day _____

17. Soccer _____

18. Paper Making _____

19. Addition _____

20. Jazz _____

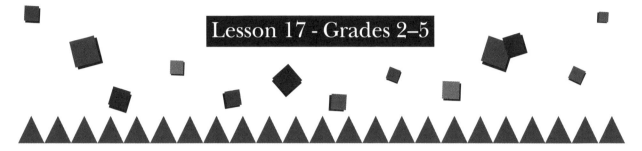

What's My Favorite Call Number?

Lesson 17 - Grades 2–5

Objective

Students will become familiar with the nonfiction section as they select a favorite call number.

Materials

• What's My Favorite Call Number? handout (page 74)

Pre-Lesson Preparation

• Copy the What's My Favorite Call Number? handout and cut into enough strips for each student to have one.

Lesson Procedure

1. Tell students that today, they will become familiar with nonfiction call numbers and choose their favorite.

2. Distribute a "What's My Favorite Call Number?" strip to each student.

3. Direct students to browse the nonfiction section, and then have them record their favorite call number on the strip. Ask them to explain why they chose that particular call number.

4. Tell students not to share their answers with any classmates.

5. Choose four students to stand in front of the class. Collect their "What's My Favorite Call Number?" strips. Read one aloud to the class, and invite students to guess which of their classmates at the front of the room chose that particular call number as his or her favorite. After several guesses, reveal the correct answer. Direct the student to sit down and choose another to take his or her place.

6. Repeat as time allows. For a fun surprise, add your own favorite call number into the mix!

What's My Favorite Call Number?

Name _____

My favorite call number is _____

because_____

_____

_____.

— — — — — — — — — — — — — — — — — — — —

Name _____

My favorite call number is _____

because_____

_____

_____.

— — — — — — — — — — — — — — — — — — — —

Name _____

My favorite call number is _____

because_____

_____

_____.

— — — — — — — — — — — — — — — — — — — —

Name _____

My favorite call number is _____

because_____

_____

_____.

— — — — — — — — — — — — — — — — — — — —

Name _____

My favorite call number is _____

because_____

_____

_____.

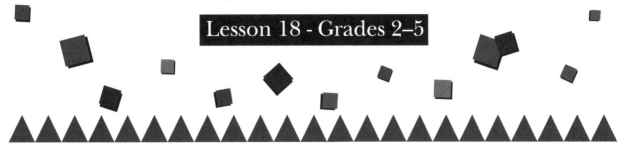

Dewey Domination

Lesson 18 - Grades 2–5

Objective

Students will review several Dewey Decimal system classifications and learn how the Dewey Decimal system is arranged.

Materials

- Dewey Domination Cards (pages 77–80)

Pre-Lesson Preparation

- Make one set of the Dewey Domination cards for each group of 3–4 students.

Lesson Procedure

1. Announce to students that today, they will need their library wits about them because they are going to play the great game of Dewey Domination.

2. Display the Dewey Domination cards for students to see. Explain that each card shows a Dewey Decimal number and the subject that the number represents. Then explain that Dewey numbers begin at 000 and continue to 999. Nonfiction books are therefore arranged numerically on the shelves, from lowest number to highest.

3. Put students into groups of 3–4. Choose one student per group to shuffle and distribute the cards face-down as evenly as possible to all players. Students should not look at their cards. Once the cards have been dealt, have students turn over their top cards at the same time. The student with the highest Dewey number wins the other cards. Before the winner collects the cards, each student must read their Dewey number and category aloud. The activity continues until all of the cards have been turned over. The student with the most cards wins the game and is the Dewey Dominator.

4. Repeat as time allows.

Extension

Dewey Line-Up Game: Put students into groups of 3–4. Cards are dealt as evenly as possible. On the count of three, each student looks at his or her cards at the same time, and then races to put his or her cards in the correct Dewey numerical order. The first student to correctly order his or her cards is the winner. Repeat as time allows.

<u>Dewey Derby:</u> Make a pile of Dewey Domination cards. Have students draw from the pile, and file the card as fast as they can in the correct spot in the nonfiction section. The winning student completes the task first. Repeat as time allows.

<u>Dewey Higher or Lower:</u> Put students into groups of 3–4. Place all of the Dewey Domination cards face-down into equal rows. Choose one student to begin by turning over the first card in the first row. Have the student guess whether the next card in the row is a lower or higher Dewey Decimal number. Ask the student to turn over the next card. If correct, the student may continue play across the row. As soon as the student makes a wrong guess, the turn passes to the next player. Repeat until all cards are turned over.

Dewey Domination Cards

510	**387.2**	**391**	**398.2**
Math	Ships	Clothing	Folk tales
415	**468**	**495.1**	**523.2**
Grammar	Spanish	Chinese	Space
551.2	**551.5**	**568**	**581**
Volcanoes	Weather	Dinosaurs	Plants

Dewey Domination Cards

629.1	**629.2**	**636.7**	**636.8**
Rockets	Trucks	Dogs	Cats
921	**943**	**972**	**973.7**
Biography	Germany	Mexico	Civil War
979.4	**971**	**940.3**	**794.6**
California	Canada	World War	Bowling

Dewey Domination Cards

340	**394.2**	**523.3**	**523.4**
Law	Holidays	Moon	Planets
523.7	**630**	**634**	**636.1**
Sun	Agriculture	Forestry	Horses
797.2	**646**	**730**	**748**
Swimming	Sewing	Sculpture	Glass

Dewey Domination Cards

597	**598.1**	**598**	**728.8**
Sharks	Reptiles	Birds	Castles
743	**780**	**793.7**	**793.8**
Drawing	Music	Puzzles	Magic
796.32	**796.33**	**608.7**	**625.1**
Basketball	Soccer	Inventions	Railroads

It's All in a Name . . . the Last Name: Biographies and Autobiographies

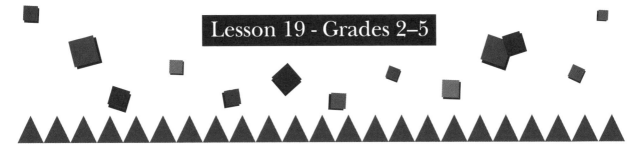

Lesson 19 - Grades 2–5

Objective

Students will learn about biographies and autobiographies and how they are shelved.

Materials

- Biography and Autobiography Call Numbers cards (page 83)
- Example biography and autobiography

Pre-Lesson Preparation

- Copy and cut out enough sets of the Biography and Autobiography Call Number cards for each group of 3–4 students to have two. They will use these two sets to play a matching game.

Lesson Procedure

1. Tell students that today, they will be learning about biographies, autobiographies, and how these books are shelved in the media center.

2. Explain the following terms to students, and then show your sample titles:

    Biography—a story about a real person's life, written by someone else.

    Autobiography—a story about a real person's life, written by that person.

3. Show students the sample biography's call number. As you point to the spine, explain that the call number helps us to find the book in the library, and that all biographies have the same call number: 921.

4. Further explain that the call number also contains the first three letters of the biography subject's last name (not the author's).

5. Tell students that biographies are arranged alphabetically by biography subjects' last names, not the authors' last names.

6. Have students practice recognizing biography call numbers and putting them in order by distributing two Biography and Autobiography Call Numbers card sets to each group. Direct students to mix both sets together, and place each card face-down. The first player will then turn over two cards so that everyone in the group can see them. If the cards match, the student keeps the pair and takes another turn. If they do not match, he or she turns them over again, and the next player takes a turn. Continue playing until all the cards are matched.

7. When all cards are matched, students put them in order as they would be found on the shelves.

Extension

*See the Fiction 7-UP lesson (page 64). You can also use this activity to put the biography call numbers in order.

Biography and Autobiography Call Numbers

Abraham Lincoln	Rosa Parks	Martin Luther King, Jr.	Benjamin Franklin
921 LIN	**921 PAR**	**921 KIN**	**921 FRA**
George Washington	Helen Keller	Susan B. Anthony	Harriet Tubman
921 WAS	**921 KEL**	**921 ANT**	**921 TUB**
Sequoyah	Cynthia Rylant	Thomas Jefferson	Michael Jordan
921 SEQ	**921 RYL**	**921 JEF**	**921 JOR**
Paul Revere	C.S. Lewis	Ray Charles	Hank Aaron
921 REV	**921 LEW**	**921 CHA**	**921 AAR**
Neil Armstrong	Alexander Graham Bell	Betsy Ross	Molly Brown
921 ARM	**921 BEL**	**921 ROS**	**921 BRO**
Annie Oakley	Clara Barton	Amelia Earhart	Thomas Edison
921 OAK	**921 BAR**	**921 EAR**	**921 EDI**

Ingredients for Success: More about Biographies and Autobiographies

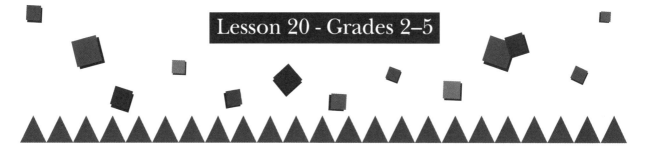

Lesson 20 - Grades 2–5

Objective

Students will learn about biographies, autobiographies, and how they are arranged in the nonfiction section.

Materials

- Ingredients For Success Biographies (pages 86–87)
- Large bowl
- Spoon
- Measuring cup
- M&Ms, Cheerios, pretzels, Goldfish crackers, and raisins
- Napkins
- Example biographies and autobiographies

Pre-Lesson Preparation

- Clean a large table for the bowl and ingredients.

Lesson Procedure

1. Explain to students that they will be learning about biographies and autobiographies and how they are arranged in the media center.

2. Explain the following terms to students, and then show your sample titles:

   Biography—a story about a real person's life written by someone else.

   Autobiography—a story about a real person's life written by that person.

3. Show students the sample biography's call number. As you point to the spine, explain that the call number helps us to find the book in the library, and that all biographies have the same call number: 921.

4. Further explain that the call number also contains the first three letters of the biography subject's last name (not the author's).

5. Tell students that biographies are arranged alphabetically by biography subjects' last names, not the authors' last names. Show some examples.

6. Tell students that a lot of biographies are written about people who have been successful in some way. Explain that today, you are all going to look at some "ingredients for success" by learning about several famous people.

7. Read the Ingredients For Success Biographies aloud. Pause after each biography, and discuss the person and what his or her "ingredient for success" was. (There may be several answers.) After each biography is read, select a student to write the call number that would correspond to the biography on the board. Be sure that these students put the call numbers in alphabetical order as they are added to the board.

8. After the biographies have been read, select one student per ingredient to measure an "ingredient for success" into the bowl. Use the recipe below:

Ingredients For Success

1 Cup of (Caring) M&Ms (Susan B. Anthony)

2 Cups of (Determined) Pretzels (Helen Keller)

1 Cup of (Courageous) Goldfish (Harriet Tubman)

1 Cup of (Respectful) Raisins (Martin Luther King, Jr.)

3 Cups of (Dedicated) Cheerios (Jim Abbott)

Mix together and serve about a ¼ cup to each student. Makes about 30 servings.

9. Tell students that these "ingredients for success" are within us all. Talk about ways they can use these attributes in their everyday lives. Enjoy the trail mix together as a reminder of the activity!

Ingredients for Success Biographies

Susan B. Anthony (1820–1906)

Susan B. Anthony spent her life fighting for equal rights for women. During this time, women did not have the right to vote. Anthony spoke out against this. In 1872, she illegally voted in the presidential election. She was arrested and fined $100, which she never paid. Fourteen years after her death, the 19th Amendment to the Constitution was ratified, which gave women the right to vote. Anthony's persistence and caring helped make this happen. In 1979 and 1980, the United States minted a $1.00 coin that had her picture on it. (Show students the coin if you have one.) Which ingredient for success do you think Susan B. Anthony had? (Caring, persistence, etc.)

Harriet Tubman (1821–1913)

Harriet Tubman was called "the Moses of her people" because she led hundreds of slaves on a secret path to freedom. Tubman was born into slavery, and in 1849, she escaped to Philadelphia. She spent her life helping other slaves escape, too. She made 19 dangerous trips to the South and helped more than 300 slaves escape to the North. There was a $40,000 reward for her capture, but she was never caught. In later years, she helped raise money for former slaves and helped to establish schools for them. She was a remarkable woman. Which ingredient for success do you think Harriet Tubman had? (Courage, independence, etc.)

Jim Abbott (1967–)

Jim Abbott was born without a right hand, but he didn't let that stop him from pursuing his dream of becoming a professional baseball player. As a child, he spent hours bouncing a ball off a wall to practice throwing. His dedication was enormous. After high school, he went to the University of Michigan on a baseball scholarship. As their pitcher, he had 26 wins and only eight losses. He helped the United States win a gold medal in baseball at the 1988 Summer Olympic Games. After the Olympics, he enjoyed a successful career with the California Angels. Which ingredient for success do you think Jim Abbott had? (Dedication, responsibility, etc.)

Ingredients for Success Biographies

Helen Keller (1880–1968)

Helen Keller fell ill when she was 19 months old, and she lost her sense of sight and hearing. A special teacher, Anne Sullivan, came to live with her when she was six years old. Anne taught Helen to spell words by using a touch system on her hand. Finally, Helen understood that the special touches on her hand spelled words. Helen went on to read Braille (if possible, show students a sample of Braille), write with a special typewriter, and speak. She graduated from Radcliffe College at age 24 and spent her life helping others who were disabled. Helen didn't let her disabilities keep her from living life to its fullest. Which ingredient for success do you think she had? (Determination, bravery, etc.)

Martin Luther King, Jr. (1929–1968)

Martin Luther King, Jr., was a civil rights leader who told African Americans to fight for equal rights with their words, not their fists. Because he promoted peaceful activism, he was given a Nobel Peace Prize in 1964. But not everybody liked what Martin Luther King, Jr., had to say. His feelings about civil rights also made many people angry. He was threatened and his house was bombed, but he didn't give up. He continued to share his message of respect, love, peace, and equality. In 1968, King was assassinated in Memphis, Tennessee. His memory and contributions to our society are honored each year on Martin Luther King, Jr., Day. Which ingredient for success do you think he had? (Respect, conviction, etc.)

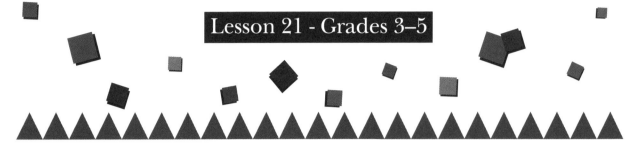

Let's Go on a Scavenger Hunt!

Lesson 21 - Grades 3–5

Objective

Students will practice finding books in the media center by participating in a scavenger hunt.

Materials

- The Great Scavenger Book Hunt handout (page 89)
- Prizes (optional)

Pre-Lesson Preparation

- Make a copy of The Great Scavenger Book Hunt handout for each student.

Lesson Procedure

1. Tell students that today, the media center is the place for the Great Scavenger Book Hunt!

2. Distribute a Great Scavenger Book Hunt handout to each student, and direct them to complete the scavenger hunt. Tell students that they must write the title and call number of the book that they select for each answer. Students may also work as partners.

3. (Optional) Award prizes, such as bookmarks, to students for completing the hunt.

4. Have students share some of the resources that they found.

The Great Scavenger Book Hunt

See if you can find . . .

1. The title and call number of a book about Martin Luther King, Jr. (hint: 921)

2. The title and call number of a fairy tale (hint: 398.2)

3. The title and call number of a sports book (hint: 796s)

4. The title and call number of a fiction book written by Cynthia Rylant

5. The title and call number of a book written by Ezra Jack Keats

6. The title and call number of a mystery book

7. The title and call number of a Magic Tree House book

8. The title and call number of a book about the solar system (hint: 520s)

9. The title and call number of a book by Leo Lioni

10. The title and call number of a nonfiction (true) book about animals (hint: 590s)

Is It Fiction or Nonfiction? That Is the Question!

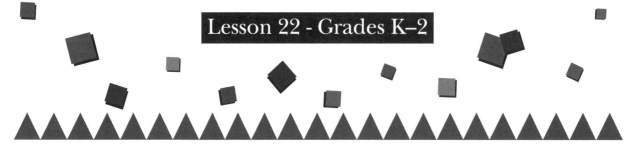

Lesson 22 - Grades K–2

Objective

Students will learn how to identify fiction and nonfiction books in the media center.

Materials

- Fiction and Nonfiction Matching Cards (page 92)
- Example fictional animal story
- Example nonfiction animal story

Pre-Lesson Preparation

- Make enough sets of the Fiction and Nonfiction Matching Cards to distribute two to groups of 3–4 in the class.

Lesson Procedure

1. Tell students that there are two types of books in the media center: fiction and nonfiction. Explain that fiction books are stories that are made-up. Nonfiction books are factual, and contain true information about actual people, places, and events.

2. Explain to students that they can learn to tell the difference between fiction and nonfiction books by looking at the title and images on the cover of the book, and by reading a few sentences and studying the images on the inside.

3. Show a fictional animal book to the students and point out the following characteristics:

   - The cover illustration may look drawn or painted.
   - The pictures in the book may look drawn or painted, and may show an unreal setting.
   - The title of the book may sound as if it is a made-up story, and not a story about factual information.

4. Read several sentences from the book aloud. Ask students whether the words sound as if they are part of a made-up story, or part of a book of true facts.

5. Show a nonfiction animal book to the students and point out the following characteristics:

   • The cover illustrations of the book may look like a photograph.

   • The images in the book look like photographs and show the person, place, or thing that the book is about in a real setting.

   • The title of the book sounds as if it is about true factual information.

6. Read several sentences from the book. Ask students whether the words sound as if they are part of a made-up story, or part of a book of true facts.

7. Put students into groups of 3–4. Distribute two sets of Fiction and Nonfiction Matching Cards to each group. Direct students to mix both sets together, and place each card face-down. The first player will then turn over two cards so that everyone in the group can see them. If the cards match, the student must tell the group whether the title and illustration is fiction or nonfiction. Then, he or she keeps the pair of cards and takes another turn. If the cards do not match, the cards are turned over again, and the next player takes a turn. Continue until all the cards are matched.

Extension

Group students in pairs. Have each pair come up with three topics for a book. Instruct them to create a fiction and nonfiction title for each of their book topics.

Fiction and Nonfiction Matching Cards

The Flying Pig

By Dixie Crane

All About Pigs

By Joe Charles

The Talking Boot

By Karen Hubbard

My Big Boots

By Nick Springs

The Walking Tree

By Ruth Anne Neuman

Tall Trees

By Marilyn Portman

The Magic Bunny

By Maureen Brent

Rabbits

By Brenda Burt

The Talking Dog

By Dale Lee

Dogs and Puppies

By Helen Owen

The Purple Bear

By Tommy Merrill

Bear and Cubs

By Linda Shipley

Fiction and Nonfiction Musical Chairs

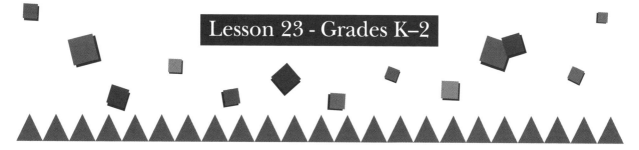

Lesson 23 - Grades K–2

Objective

Students will learn how to identify fiction and nonfiction books in the media center.

Materials

- Chairs
- Music
- Several examples of fiction and nonfiction animal books.

Pre-Lesson Preparation

- Place enough chairs in a circle for each student.
- Place a fiction or nonfiction animal book on each chair.

Lesson Procedure

1. Tell students that there are two types of books in the media center: fiction and nonfiction. Explain that fiction books are stories that are made-up. Nonfiction books are factual and contain true information about actual people, places, and events.

2. Explain to students that they can learn to tell the difference between fiction and nonfiction books by looking at the title and illustrations on the cover of the book, and by reading some of the sentences in it.

3. Show a fictional animal book to the students and point out the following characteristics:

   - The cover illustration may look drawn or painted.
   - The pictures in the book may look drawn or painted, and may show an unreal setting.
   - The title of the book may sound as if it is a made-up story, and not a story about factual information.

4. Read several sentences from the book aloud. Ask students whether the words sound as if they are part of a made-up story, or part of a book of true facts.

5. Show a nonfiction animal book to the students and point out the following characteristics:

   - The cover illustrations of the book may look like a photograph.

   - The images in the book look like photographs and show the person, place, or thing that the book is about in a real setting.

   - The title of the book sounds as if it is about true factual information.

6. Read several sentences from the book. Ask students whether the words sound as if they are part of a made-up story, or part of a book of true facts.

7. Have students practice identifying fiction and nonfiction titles by playing fiction and nonfiction musical chairs.

   - Put enough chairs in a circle so that each student has a seat.

   - Place a fiction or nonfiction book on each chair. Fiction and nonfiction animal books are a good choice. Try to put out examples of nonfiction books illustrated with drawings or paintings, in addition to photographs.

   - Direct students to walk in a circle in front of the chairs while music is played. When the music stops, students should sit in the chair closest to them. Give them a few seconds to decide whether the book in their chair is fiction or nonfiction. Then, ask all students who have a nonfiction book to hold up their books. Then, ask for all students who have a fiction book to hold up their books. Check their answers. Discuss the fact that not all nonfiction books use photographs for their work, and that it is always important to read a few sentences inside the book to make a final decision as to whether the book is fiction or nonfiction.

Extension

Use this musical chairs activity to discuss different genres of literature with grades 3–5. Instead of using the categories of fiction and nonfiction, put folktales, mysteries, biographies, etc., on the chairs and play on!

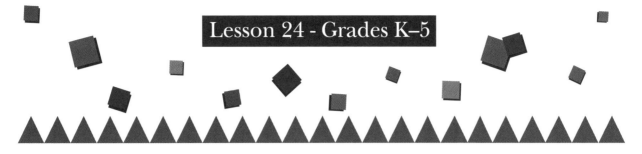

Let's Talk about It!

Lesson 24 - Grades K–5

Objective

Students will use the Question Cube to discuss a story after it has been read.

Materials

- Question Cube (page 97)

Pre-Lesson Preparation

- Write Thinking Questions from the list below on the cube. On five of the squares, write two questions. On the sixth square, write three silly directions (e.g., make a silly face, stand on one foot, etc.). Cut out, fold, and tape the cube together.

Thinking Questions

- What is the setting of the story?
- Who were the characters in the story?
- What happened in the story?
- What was the problem in the story?
- What was the solution in the story?
- Why do you think the author wrote the book?
- Has anything like this ever happened to you?
- Does this story remind you of another one?
- Did you like the story? Why or why not?
- Choose another title for the story.

Lesson Procedure

1. Use the Question Cube to discuss a story with students.

2. Show students the Question Cube. Explain that there are questions on five sides of the cube that will help you discuss the story, but warn them that there is a silly side to the Question Cube! Choose a student to roll the cube. If the student rolls a side with questions, he or she may select one to answer. If the student lands on the silly directions, he or she must select one direction to follow.

3. Continue as time allows.

Extension

*Reproduce the Question Cube template for older students to make their own cubes. Have them write open-ended questions on each side, such as:

- My favorite book is ____ because . . .
- My favorite illustrator is ____ because . . .
- My favorite author is ____ because . . .
- My favorite genre is ____ because . . .
- The scariest book I ever read was ____ because . . .
- The funniest book I ever read was ____ because . . .

Tell students to take their cubes home and use them throughout the year. Do their answers change as they read more books?

*Get students talking about books with an open-ended Question Cube. Create the cube as described above, and select one student in the class to roll it. When it settles on one side, have the student read the question aloud for you to answer. Then, roll it for the student to answer a new question. Play with several students each time you meet until every member of the class has had a turn.

Question Cube

Enlarge as needed.

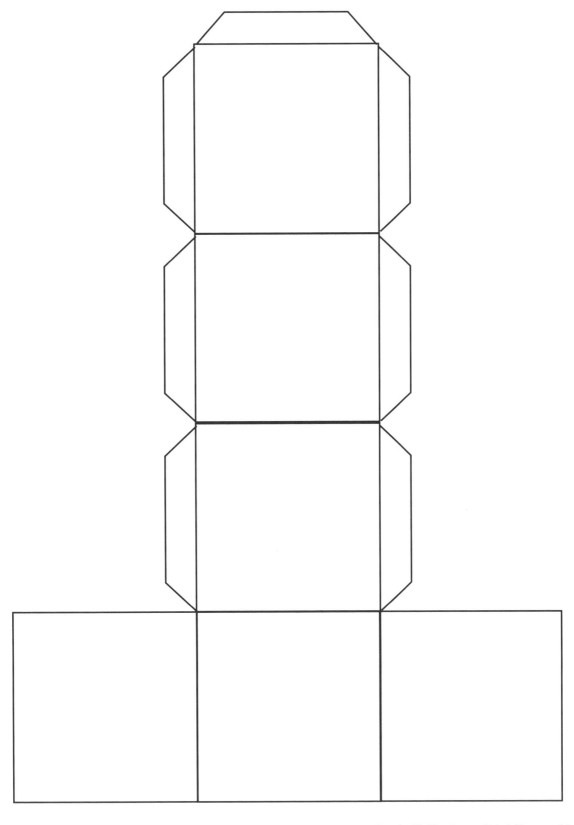

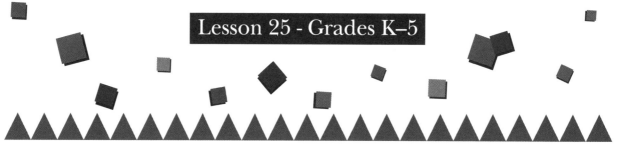

Ball of Knowledge

Lesson 25 - Grades K–5

Objective

Students will use the Ball of Knowledge to discuss a story after it has been read.

Materials

- Medium-sized plastic ball or beach ball
- Ball of Knowledge Actions and Discussion Questions (page 99)
- Marker

Pre-Lesson Preparation

- Purchase ball, if necessary
- Write the Ball of Knowledge actions and questions on the ball.

Lesson Procedure

1. Read a story aloud to the class. When you finish, direct students to stand in a circle and show them the Ball of Knowledge. Explain that there are questions on the ball that will assist them with discussing the story. In addition, tell students that there is an action that accompanies each question. Provide an example from the ball.

2. Tell students that you are going to throw the ball to someone in the circle. When the ball is caught, the student must close his or her eyes and put an index finger somewhere on the ball. The student should then perform the action and answer the question that appears closest to his or her finger.

3. After the action and question are completed, play continues when the student throws the ball to someone else.

Extension

Host a picnic (or snack) storytime outside on a beautiful day, and play with the Ball of Knowledge when you are done reading!

Ball of Knowledge Actions and Discussion Questions

- Sing the name of one of the characters.

- Do five jumping jacks and then describe what the book is about.

- Hop on one foot while you tell the solution to the story.

- Skip around the circle and then describe the problem in the story.

- Pat your head and rub your stomach while you think of another title for the story.

- Walk backwards around the circle and tell the group if something like what happened in the story has ever happened to you. Explain.

- Stand next to someone wearing blue and tell the group if this story reminds you of another story. If so, which one?

- Walk like a duck while telling the setting of the story.

- Make a funny face, then describe your favorite part of the story.

- Change places with someone in the circle and say why you think the author wrote the story.

- Whistle three times and tell if you liked the story. Why or why not?

- Spin around five times and then tell if you would recommend this story. Why or why not?

Let's Learn about the Title and Copyright Pages

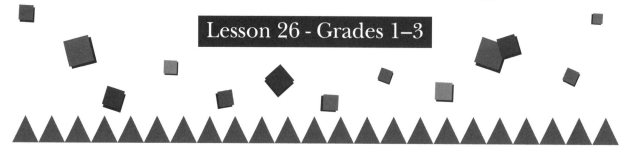

Lesson 26 - Grades 1–3

Objective

Students will learn about the information found on the title page and copyright page.

Materials

- Title Page and Copyright Page Example handout (page 102)
- Crayons
- A sample picture book for each student
- Title Page and Copyright Page Directions (page 103)
- Title Page and Copyright Page Practice (page 104)
- Overhead projector or document camera

Pre-Lesson Preparation

- Make a copy of the Title Page and Copyright Page handout for each student.
- Select enough picture books for each student to practice with one.
- Make one copy of the Title Page and Copyright Page directions.
- Make one copy of the Title Page and Copyright Page Example.

Lesson Procedure

1. Explain to students that there is a special page in a book called a title page. The title page is the first page of a book, and it contains some important information.

2. Display the Title Page and Copyright Page Example on a document camera or overhead projector.

3. Point to the following information on the example and explain its purpose:

   Title: the name of the book

   Author: the person who wrote the book

Illustrator: the person who drew the pictures in the book

Publisher: the group of people who put the book together, printed copies of it, and sent it to bookstores and libraries

Place of Publication: the city where the publisher works and puts the book together

4. Distribute a picture book to each student. Direct them to find the title page. Ask students to point to the title, author, illustrator, publisher, and place of publication. Assist as needed.

5. Tell students that there is another special page in the book called the copyright page. Explain that it is almost always found on the back of the title page, and sometimes, in the back of the book.

6. Using the example, show students the copyright page and explain the following information:

Copyright Date: The copyright date is the book's birthday. It is the year the book was printed.

Copyright Symbol: The circled, lowercase "c" that precedes the date on the copyright page. This symbol is another way of writing "copyright."

7. Direct students to find the copyright page in their book. Assist as needed.

8. Then, distribute the Title Page and Copyright Page practice handout and crayons to each student. Direct students to follow the Title Page and Copyright Page Directions, which you will read aloud. Tell them that you will only read each direction once, so they have to be good listeners.

Title Page and Copyright Page Example

Title Page   Copyright Page

The Bright Moon

by

Adam Hayes

Illustrated by

Janna Till

Copyright © 2007 by Adam Hayes

Bee Publishing

Chicago

Title Page and Copyright Page Directions

- In box 1, underline the title of the book with an orange crayon.

- In box 2, put a circle around the author's name with a blue crayon.

- In box 3, put a rectangle around the word "copyright" with a purple crayon.

- In box 4, circle the copyright date with a green crayon.

- In box 5, draw a smiley face beside the title of the book with a yellow crayon.

- In box 6, circle the city where the book was published.

- In box 7, put a line through the illustrator's name with a red crayon.

- In box 8, use a blue crayon to put an X by the city where the book was published.

- In box 9, put a star beside the publisher's name with an orange crayon.

Title Page and Copyright Page Practice

1
I Love Summer
by
Joe Adams
Illustrated by
Jan Peak

Pine Press
New York

2
The Fun Monkey
by
Brenda Penn
Illustrated by
Kayla Edwin

Erica Publishing
Chicago

3

Copyright © 2005
by Leaf Press

4

Copyright © 2007
by Cassidee Press

5
The Big Box
by
Crista Bryson
Illustrated by
Pablo Flores

Milford Publishing
Charlotte

6
The Mouse
by
Ada Barton
Illustrated by
Simia Jackson

Rainy Press
Los Angeles

7
The River
by
Chris Sparks
Illustrated by
Ben Flynn

Poplar Publishing
Austin

8
My Puppy
by
Anna Bee
Illustrated by
Alex Monk

Jones Press
Baltimore

9
Hippo's Birthday
by
Ashby Gale
Illustrated by
Jenny Scott

Art Press
Brevard

All about the Title Page and the Copyright Page

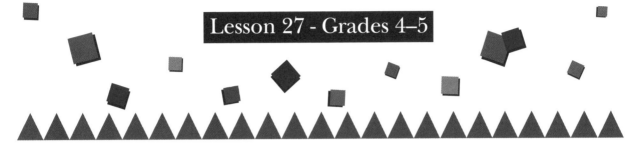

Lesson 27 - Grades 4–5

Objective

Students will learn about the information found on the title page and copyright page.

Materials

- A Title Page and Copyright Page Example (page 107)
- All about the Title Page and Copyright Page handout (page 108)
- Pencils

Pre-Lesson Preparation

- Make a copy of the All about the Title Page and the Copyright Page handout for each student.
- Make one copy of A Title Page and the Copyright Page Example.
- Choose enough nonfiction books for each student to have one.

Lesson Procedure

1. Explain to students that there is a special page in a book called a title page. The title page is the first page of a book, and it contains some important information.

2. Show students A Title Page and Copyright Page Example on a document camera or overhead projector.

3. Point to the following information on the example and explain its purpose:

   <u>Title</u>: the name of the book

   <u>Author</u>: the person who wrote the book

   <u>Illustrator</u>: the person who made pictures for the book

   <u>Publisher</u>: the group of people who put the book together, printed copies of it, and sent it to bookstores and libraries

Place of Publication: the city where the publisher works and puts the book together

4. Distribute a nonfiction book to each student. Direct them to find the title page. Ask students to point to the title, author, illustrator, publisher, and place of publication. Assist as needed.

5. Tell students that there is another special page in the book called the copyright page. Explain that it is almost always found on the back of the title page, and sometimes, in the back of the book.

6. Using the example, show students the copyright page and explain the following information:

   Copyright Date: The copyright date is the book's birthday.

   Copyright Symbol: The circled, lowercase "c" that precedes the date on the copyright page. This symbol is another way of writing "copyright."

7. Explain that the copyright date is important when doing research. If students want to find the latest, most up-to-date information about a topic, then they should look at the most recent books available. The copyright date will tell them how recently a book was published.

8. Ask students which book would be the best choice if they were doing a report on planets:

   All about the Planets (Copyright 1964) or The Planets (Copyright 2007).

   Emphasize again that the book published in 2007 would have the latest information about the topic.

9. Direct students to find the copyright page in their book. Assist as needed. Ask students to identify the copyright date on their books. See whose book is the oldest or the newest.

10. Have students practice finding information on the title page and copyright page by giving them the All about the Title Page and Copyright Page handout to complete.

11. Discuss answers as a class.

A Title Page and Copyright Page Example

Title Page

Copyright Page

The Moon

by
Julia Wilder
Illustrated by
Tim Gatsby

Copyright © 2007 by Julia Wilder

Camp Publishing
Chicago

Which copyright date is better for research?

☐ All About the Planets (copyright 1964)   ☐ The Planets (copyright 2007)

All about the Title Page and Copyright Page

Title Page   Copyright Page

The Sun By Janet Hubbard Illustrated by Ron Waters Oak Press Chicago	 Copyright © 2006 by Janet Hubbard

1. When was the book published? _____

2. What is the title of the book? _____

3. What is the name of the publishing company? _____

4. Who is the illustrator of the book? _____

5. What is the name of the city where the book was published? _____

6. What is the name of the author of the book? _____

7. What does © mean? _____

8. Why is the copyright date important? _____

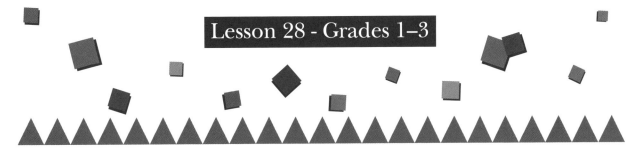

Let's Learn about the Table of Contents

Lesson 28 - Grades 1–3

Objective

Students will learn about the information found in the table of contents.

Materials

- Using the Table of Contents handout (page 110)
- Using the Table of Contents Directions and Answer Key (page 111)
- Nonfiction books that include a table of contents
- Pencils

Pre-Lesson Preparation

- Make a copy of the Using the Table of Contents handout for each student.
- Make one copy of the Using the Table of Contents Directions and Answer Key.
- Select a simple nonfiction book for the lesson and pull enough simple nonfiction books for each student to have one.

Lesson Procedure

1. Explain to students that there is a special page in a book called the table of contents. The table of contents is usually the second page of the book, and it contains important information.

2. Using the selected nonfiction book, show students the table of contents.

3. Explain that the table of contents lists the titles of each chapter in the book. Chapter titles contain important words that can help you understand what each chapter is about. Discuss using an example from your sample book.

4. Further explain that beside each chapter title is a page number, which shows where in the book the chapter begins.

5. Distribute a sample nonfiction book to each student. Direct them to find the table of contents. Then, ask students to practice reading the chapter titles, and find those chapters in the book using the page numbers listed in the table of contents.

6. Now distribute the Using the Table of Contents handouts to the class. Direct students to follow the directions, which you will read aloud. Tell them that you will only read each direction once, so they must be good listeners.

Using the Table of Contents

BOX 1

Table of Contents

BOX 2

Table of Contents

Using the Table of Contents Directions and Answer Key

- In box 1, put a circle around the page number where you can find information about how to train your dog. (Page 7)

- In box 1, underline the chapter title that is about what dogs eat. (Chapter 2: What dogs eat)

- In box 1, put a check by the chapter number that is about exercising your dog. (Chapter 5)

- In box 1, put a smiley face by the page number where you can find information about how to care for your dog. (Page 5)

- In box 2, underline the chapter title that is about what makes it snow. (Chapter 2: What makes it snow?)

- In box 2, circle the page number where you can find out information about rain. (Page 1)

- In box 2, put a smiley face by the chapter number that is about clouds. (Chapter 3)

- In box 2, write your name under the chapter title that is about wind. (Chapter 4)

Check Out the Table of Contents!

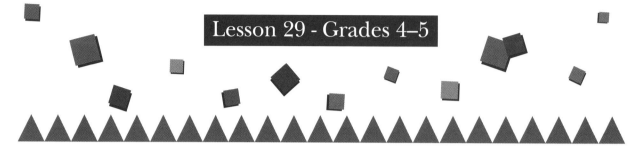

Lesson 29 - Grades 4–5

Objective

Students will learn about the information found in the table of contents.

Materials

- Check Out the Table of Contents! handout (page 113)
- Pencils

Pre-Lesson Preparation

- Make a copy of the Check Out the Table of Contents! handout for each student.
- Select a nonfiction book for the lesson and pull enough nonfiction books for each student to have one.

Lesson Procedure

1. Explain to students that there is a special page in a book called the Table of Contents. The table of contents is usually the second page of the book, and it contains important information.

2. Using the selected nonfiction book, show students the table of contents.

3. Explain that the table of contents lists the titles of each chapter in the book. Chapter titles contain important words that can help you understand what each chapter is about. Discuss using an example from your sample book.

4. Further explain that beside each chapter title is a page number, which shows where in the book the chapter begins.

5. Distribute a sample nonfiction book to each student. Direct them to find the table of contents. Then, ask students to practice reading the chapter titles, and find those chapters in the book using the page numbers listed in the table of contents.

6. Now have students practice by answering the questions on the Check Out the Table of Contents! handout.

7. When students have finished, discuss their answers.

Check Out the Table of Contents!

Table of Contents

1. Which chapter number would help you find out if an eagle can live to be 25 years of age? _____

2. On which page could you find out how many babies a mother eagle has? _____

3. Which chapter would tell you if an eagle likes to eat fish? _____

4. Which chapter would tell you if eagles like to be around other eagles? _____

5. Would any of these chapters tell you about famous eagle symbols? _____

6. Which chapter would help you find out if a hawk is related to an eagle, and on which page does that chapter begin? _____, _____

7. Which chapter would help you find out how far an eagle can see? _____

8. Which chapter would tell you the color of eagle feathers? _____

Check Out the Table of Contents!

Answer Key

1. Which chapter number would help you find out if an eagle can live to be 25 years of age? (Chapter 10)

2. On which page could you find out how many babies a mother eagle has? (Page 21)

3. Which chapter would tell you if an eagle likes to eat fish? Do all eagles eat the same food? (Chapter 5)

4. Which chapter would tell you if eagles like to be around other eagles? (Chapter 7)

5. Would any of these chapters tell you about famous eagle symbols? (No.)

6. Which chapter would help you find out if a hawk is related to an eagle, and on which page does that chapter begin? (Chapter 2, page 5)

7. Which chapter would help you find out how far an eagle can see?(Chapter 6)

8. Which chapter would tell you the color of eagle feathers? (Chapter 4)

The Glossary Helps Us Learn New Words!

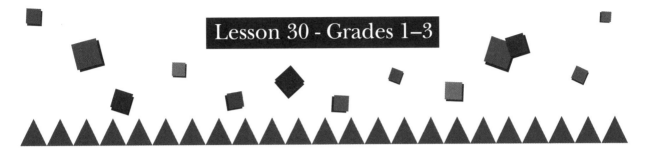

Lesson 30 - Grades 1–3

Objective

Students will learn how to use a glossary.

Materials

- The Glossary handout (page 116)
- The Glossary Directions and Answer Key (page 117)
- Sample nonfiction books that include a glossary
- Pencils

Pre-Lesson Preparation

- Make a copy of The Glossary handout for each student.
- Make one copy of The Glossary Directions.
- Choose a simple nonfiction book for the lesson and pull enough simple nonfiction books for each student to have one. Titles should include a glossary.

Lesson Procedure

1. Explain to students that some books contain a special section called a glossary. The glossary is found at the back of the book.

2. Show students the glossary in your sample nonfiction book.

3. Explain that the glossary is like a small dictionary. It defines new, unfamiliar vocabulary words that appear in the book. If you are confused about the meaning of a word as you are reading, check the glossary for the definition. The words are listed in alphabetical order.

4. Distribute a nonfiction book to each student. Direct them to find the glossary. Then ask students to select a word from the glossary and read its definition. Choose a few students to share the word they read.

5. Next, distribute The Glossary handout, and instruct students to follow the directions as you read them aloud. Tell them that you will only read each direction once, so they must be good listeners.

6. When the class has completed the handout, discuss the answers.

The Glossary

Glossary

Forest—land that is covered mostly by trees

Groom—to clean

Hunt—to find and kill other animals for food

Insect—a small animal with six legs, three body sections, and two antennas

Meadow—a large, open field of grass

Nest—a cozy place or shelter

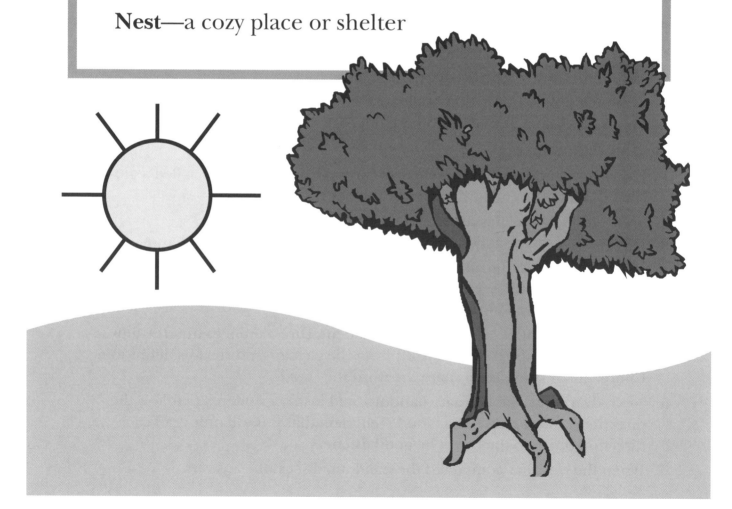

The Glossary
Directions and Answer Key

1. Put a smiley by the glossary word that means a "cozy shelter."
   (Nest)

2. Underline the glossary word that means "to find and kill other animals for food."
   (Hunt)

3. Circle the glossary word that rhymes with "broom."
   (Groom)

4. Put a square around the glossary word that comes after the word "Hunt."
   (Insect)

5. Circle the number of legs that an insect has on its body.
   (Six)

6. Draw a star by the word that means "land that is covered mostly by trees."
   (Forest)

7. Put a star by the glossary word that means a large, open field of grass.
   (Meadow)

8. Write your name by your favorite definition.
   (All answers are correct.)

What's in the Glossary?

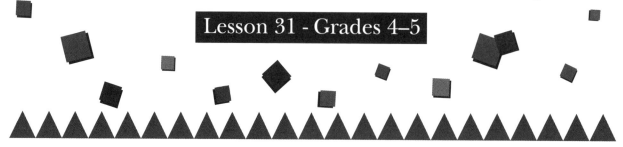

Lesson 31 - Grades 4–5

Objective

Students will learn about the information found in the glossary.

Materials

- What's in the Glossary? handout (page 119)
- Sample nonfiction books that include a glossary
- Pencils

Pre-Lesson Preparation

- Make a copy of the What's in the Glossary? handout for each student.
- Select a nonfiction book for the lesson and pull enough nonfiction books for each student to have one. Titles should include a glossary.

Lesson Procedure

1. Explain to students that some books contain a special section called a glossary. The glossary is found at the back of the book.

2. Show students the glossary in your sample nonfiction book.

3. Explain that the glossary is like a small dictionary. It defines new, unfamiliar vocabulary words that appear in the book. If you are confused about the meaning of a word as you are reading, check the glossary for the definition. The words are listed in alphabetical order.

4. Distribute a nonfiction book to each student. Direct them to find the glossary. Then ask students to select a word from the glossary and read its definition. Choose a few students to share the words they read.

5. Distribute the What's in the Glossary? handout and direct students to complete.

6. Discuss the answers as a class.

What's in the Glossary?

Glossary

Brood—To sit on eggs to keep them warm until they hatch

Down—Fluffy feathers

Eaglet—Baby eagle

Egg Tooth—A hard point on the top of an eaglet's beak that helps them break through their shell

Hatch—To come out of an egg

Molt—To lose old feathers and grow new ones

Prey—An animal that is hunted by another animal

Talons—Claws of an eagle

1. How are words listed in the glossary? _____

2. Why is a glossary important in a book? _____
   _____

3. Does an eaglet use its feet to break out of its shell? _____
   _____

4. What does the word "talons" mean? _____

5. Do cats have down? _____

6. Can people molt? _____

7. Write a sentence using the word "prey." _____
   _____

8. What is a newborn eagle called? _____

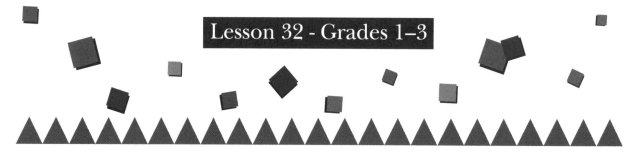

What Is the Index?

Lesson 32 - Grades 1–3

Objective

Students will learn about the index and practice using it.

Materials

- The Index Helps Me handout (page 121)
- The Index Helps Me Directions and Answer Key (page 122)
- Sample nonfiction books that include an index
- Pencils

Pre-Lesson Preparation

- Make a copy of The Index Helps Me handout for each student.
- Make one copy of The Index Helps Me Directions and Answer Key.
- Choose a simple nonfiction book for the lesson and pull enough simple nonfiction books for each student to have one. Titles should include an index.

Lesson Procedure

1. Explain to students that some books contain a special section called an index. The index is usually the last section or page in the book.

2. Using the selected nonfiction book, show students the index.

3. Explain that the index lists all of the subjects found in the book. The subjects are listed in alphabetical order. The pages where the subjects can be found are also listed. Demonstrate how to look up a subject in the index.

4. Distribute a nonfiction book to each student. Direct them to find the index, and have them practice looking up a few subjects.

5. Then, distribute The Index Helps Me handout. Instruct students to follow the directions that you are about to read aloud. Tell them that you will only read each direction once, so they must be good listeners.

6. When the class completes the activity, discuss the answers.

The Index Helps Me

Index

Beak, 3

Chirping, 4

Eyes, 7

Feathers, 8, 9

Flying, 10

Legs, 11

Size, 12

Wings, 14, 15

The Index Helps Me
Directions and Answer Key

Follow the directions as they are read aloud.

1. Circle the page numbers where you would read about wings.
   (14, 15)

2. Draw a line under the page number where you would read about chirping. (4)

3. Put a check by the page number where you would read about eyes.
   (7)

4. Put a triangle around the page number where you would read about flying.
   (10)

5. Put a smiley face by the page number where you would read about beaks.
   (3)

6. Put a square around the page number where you would read about size.
   (12)

7. Put a rectangle around the page numbers where you would read about feathers.
   (8, 9)

8. At the bottom of the page, write the name of the subject you would like to read about. (All answers are correct.)

9. At the bottom of the page, write the page number where you would find how much an eagle weighs.
   (12)

10. At the bottom of the page, write the page number where you would find out how far an eagle can see.
    (7)

Tell Me More about the Index

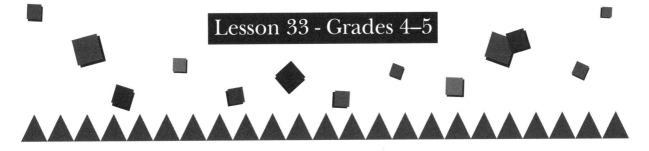

Lesson 33 - Grades 4–5

Objective

Students will learn more about the information found in the index.

Materials

- Look in the Index handout (page 124)
- Pencils
- Sample nonfiction books that include an index

Pre-Lesson Preparation

- Make a copy of the Look in the Index handout for each student.
- Choose a nonfiction book for the lesson and pull enough nonfiction books for each student to have one. Titles should include an index.

Lesson Procedure

1. Explain to students that some books contain a special section called an index. The index is usually the last section or page in the book.

2. Using the selected nonfiction book, show students the index.

3. Explain that the index lists all of the subjects found in the book. The subjects are listed in alphabetical order. The pages where the subjects can be found are also listed.

4. Next, explain to students that sometimes, main subject headings will list subheadings underneath them. Demonstrate how to look up a subject in the index.

5. Distribute a nonfiction book to each student. Direct them to find the index, and ask them to practice looking up a few subjects.

6. Next, distribute the Look in the Index handout and direct students to complete. When students are finished, discuss the answers as a class.

Look in the Index

Index

Bald Eagle

color, 3,4

diet, 5

nest, 6

birds of prey, 7

young, 9,10

Golden Eagle

eyelids, 11

habitat, 12,13

relatives, 14

size, 15

wings, 17,23,25

Which page number(s) will direct you to the answers to these questions? Use the index above to fill in the blanks.

1. Is the hawk related to the Golden Eagle? Page(s) _____

2. Does the Golden Eagle have a clear eyelid? Page(s) _____

3. What color is the Bald Eagle? Page(s) _____

4. How many eggs does the Bald Eagle hatch? Page(s) _____

5. Does the Bald Eagle eat fish? Page(s) _____

6. Does the Golden Eagle live in North America? Page(s) _____

7. Where does a Bald Eagle build its nest? Page(s) _____

8. How much does the Golden Eagle weigh? Page(s) _____

9. How does the Golden Eagle fly? Page(s) _____

10. What is a bird of prey? Page(s) _____

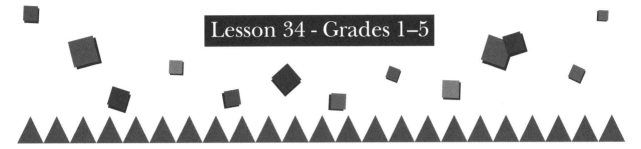

Musical Parts: Parts of a Book Review

Lesson 34 - Grades 1–5

Objective

Students will review the parts of a book.

Materials

- Parts of a Book Cube (page 127)
- Tape/CD Player and children's music

Pre-Lesson Preparation

- Make one copy of the Parts of a Book Cube; cut out, and assemble.
- Select a nonfiction book for the lesson.
- Select several nonfiction books for students to use during the lesson.

Lesson Procedure

1. Tell students that they are going to review the parts of a book.

2. Review the following parts of a book with the students. Point to the appropriate page in the selected nonfiction book as you explain the parts.

   Title Page: Tells you the title (name of the book), the author (person who wrote the book), the illustrator (person who made the pictures), the publisher (person who put the book together), and place of publication (city where the book was made).

   Cover: Protects the pages and tells us the title of the book, the author's name, and the illustrator's name.

   Spine: Holds the pages together and tells us the call number (the book's address in the library).

   Table of Contents: Lists all of the chapter titles in the book.

   Glossary: Mini dictionary that alphabetically lists and defines new, unfamiliar words in the book.

<u>Index</u>: Alphabetically lists all of the subjects found in the book, and page numbers where each subject can be found.

3. Have students review the parts of a book by participating in "Musical Parts." Direct students to sit in a circle. Place several nonfiction books in the middle of the circle. Show students the Parts of a Book Cube. Tell students that they are going to pass the cube around the circle while music is played. When the music stops, direct the student with the cube to roll it. When the cube settles, the student will read the term that is rolled aloud, and select a nonfiction book from the middle of the circle. Then, he or she must identify that part of the book.

4. Continue as time allows.

Extension

*Challenge older students by designating two teams during Musical Parts (students in the circle can count off 1, 2, 1, 2). When the cube is rolled, the rolling student will challenge another student on the opposite team to race to find the correct page in one of the books from the middle of the circle. You will tell them when to begin. The team who correctly identifies the part of the book first wins one point. Any rough treatment of books is an automatic three-point deduction.

*Make enough copies of the Parts of a Book Cube for each student, and help them assemble their cubes. Provide small stickers, etc., for decorating. Students may take their cubes with them as a reminder of the lesson and for further practice at home.

Parts of a Book Cube

Enlarge as needed.

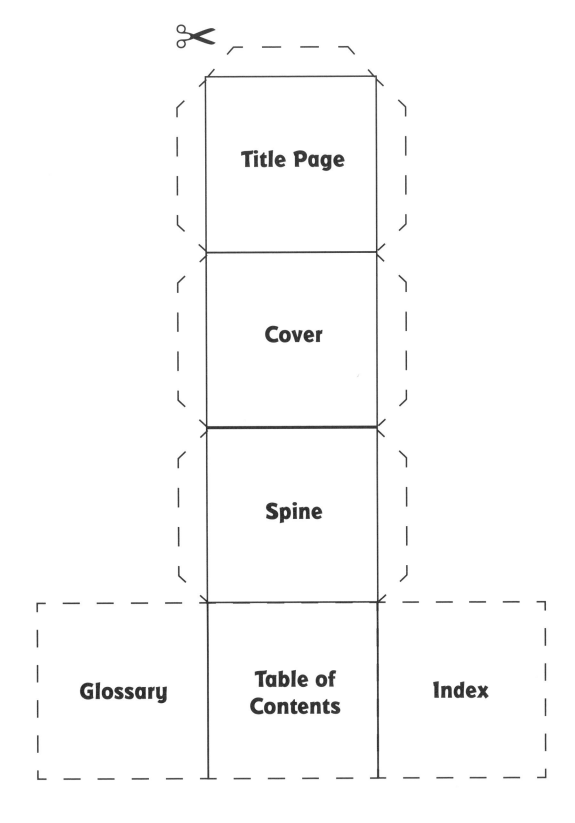

Title Page

Cover

Spine

Glossary

Table of Contents

Index

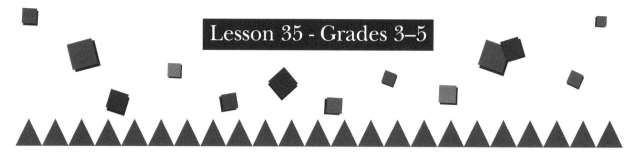

The Caldecott Medal

Lesson 35 - Grades 3–5

Objective

Students will learn about the Caldecott Medal.

Materials

- Caldecott Bingo handout (page 130)
- Caldecott-Winning titles list (pages 131–133)
- Bingo pieces (buttons, small squares of paper, etc.)
- Prizes (optional)

Pre-Lesson Preparation

- Make several copies of the Caldecott-Winning Titles list for students to share. Students will refer to the list when writing titles on their Caldecott Bingo handout.

- Make a copy of the Caldecott Bingo handout for each student.

- Make one copy of the Caldecott-Wining Titles list and cut into strips. Place strips in envelope.

Lesson Procedure

1. Explain to students that each year, a special medal is awarded to an illustrator of an outstanding picture book. It is called the Caldecott Award. Explain the following facts about the award:

   - The Caldecott is given each year to an illustrator of the most distinguished American picture book for children published the preceding year.

   - The award is named after Randolph Caldecott, a famous English illustrator.

   - The winner must be an American citizen or resident of the United States.

   - The first award was given in 1938 to Dorothy Lathrop for her illustrations in the book, <u>Animals of the Bible</u>. The most recent award was given last year to (provide name of illustrator and title).

   - Some illustrators win "second" place, a Caldecott Honor, for their outstanding work.

2. Tell students that they are going to get to know some of these great picture books by playing Caldecott Bingo!

3. Distribute a Caldecott Bingo handout to each student. Distribute the Caldecott-Winning Titles list to every few students to share. Students should refer to the list as they write one title per square on their Bingo boards.

4. Draw a title strip from your envelope and read it aloud. If students have that title on their board, direct them to cover the square with a Bingo piece. The first student to complete a row horizontally, vertically, or diagonally, wins.

5. (Optional) Give a prize, such as a bookmark, to the winning student.

6. Play again as time allows.

Extension

Allow your Caldecott Bingo winners to each select one Caldecott-winning picture book from the list. Read those stories aloud the next time you meet and have students discuss why they think the books won the award.

Select a Caldecott-winning title and two Caldecott Honor books, all from the same year. Shield the jackets so students cannot see which book won what award. Read the books and allow students to vote on the one they think was the winner, and discuss why.

Caldecott Bingo

Place the book title of a Caldecott Award winner in each square.

Caldecott-Winning Titles

- *The House in the Night* by Susan Marie Swanson, illustrated by Beth Krommes, 2009

- *The Invention of Hugo Cabret* by Brian Selznick, 2008

- *Flotsam* by David Wiesner, 2007

- *The Hello Goodbye Window,* by Norton Juster, illustrated by Chris Raschka

- *Kitten's First Full Moon* by Kevin Henkes, 2005

- *The Man Who Walked Between Towers* by Mordicai Gerstein, 2004

- *My Friend Rabbit* by Eric Rohmann, 2003.

- *The Three Pigs* by David Wiesner, 2002

- *So You Want to Be President?* by Judith St. George, illustrated by David Small, 2001

- *Joseph Had a Little Overcoat* by Simms Taback, 2000

- *Snowflake Bentley* by Jacqueline Briggs Martin, illustrated by Mary Azarian, 1999

- *Rapunzel* by Paul O. Zelinsky, 1998

- *Golem* by David Wisniewski, 1997

- *Officer Buckle and Gloria* by Peggy Rathmann, 1996

- *Smoky Night* by Eve Bunting, illustrated by David Diaz, 1995

- *Grandfather's Journey* by Allen Say, 1994

- *Mirette on the High Wire* by Emily Arnold McCully, 1993

- *Tuesday* by David Wiesner, 1992

- *Black and White* by David Macaulay, 1991

- *Lon Po Po: A Red Riding Hood Story from China* by Ed Young, 1990

- *Song and Dance Man* by Karen Ackerman, illustrated by Stephen Gammell, 1989

- *Owl Moon* by Jane Yolen, illustrated by John Schoenherr, 1988

- *Hey, Al* by Arthur Yorinks, illustrated by Richard Egielski, 1987

- *The Polar Express* by Chris Van Allsburg, 1986

- *Saint George and the Dragon* by Margaret Hodges, illustrated by Trina Schart Hyman, 1985

- *The Glorious Flight, Across the Channel with Louis Bleriot* by Alice and Martin Provensen, 1984

- *Shadow* by Marcia Brown, 1983

- *Jumanji* by Chris Van Allsburg, 1982

- *Fables* by Arnold Lobel, 1981

- *Ox-Cart Man* by Donald Hall, illustrated by Barbara Cooney, 1980

- *The Girl Who Loved Wild Horses* by Paul Goble, 1979

- *Noah's Ark* by Peter Spier, 1978

- *Ashanti to Zulu: African Traditions* by Margaret Musgrove, illustrated by Leo and Diane Dillon, 1977

- *Why Mosquitoes Buzz in People's Ears* by Verna Aardema, illustrated by Leo and Diane Dillon, 1976

- *Arrow to the Sun* by Gerald McDermott, 1975

- *Duffy and the Devil* by Harve Zemach, illustrated by Margot Zemach, 1974

- *The Funny Little Woman* by Arlene Mosel, illustrated by Blair Lent, 1973

- *One Fine Day* by Nonny Hogrogian, 1972

- *A Story, A Story* by Gail E. Haley, 1971

- *Sylvester and the Magic Pebble* by William Steig, 1970

- *The Fool of the World and the Flying Ship* by Arthur Ransome, illustrated by Uri Shulevitz, 1969

- *Drummer Hoff,* Barbara Emberley, illustrated by Ed Emberley, 1968

- *Sam, Bangs, and Moonshine* by Evaline Ness, 1967

- *Always Room for One More* by Sorche Nic Leodhas, illustrated by Nonny Hogrogian, 1966

- *May I Bring a Friend?* by Beatrice Schenk de Regniers, illustrated by Beni Montresor, 1965

- *Where the Wild Things Are* by Maurice Sendak, 1964

- *The Snowy Day* by Ezra Jack Keats, 1963

- *Once a Mouse* by Marcia Brown, 1962

- *Baboushka and the Three Kings* by Ruth Robbins, illustrated by Nicolas Sidjakov, 1961

- *Nine Days to Christmas* by Marie Hall Ets and Aurora Labastida, illustrated by Marie Hall Ets, 1960

- *Chanticleer and the Fox* by Barbara Cooney, 1959

- *Time of Wonder* by Robert McCloskey, 1958

- *A Tree Is Nice* by Janice Udry, illustrated by Marc Simont, 1957

- *Frog Went A-Courtin'* by John Langstaff, illustrated by Feodor Rojankovsky, 1956

- *Cinderella, or the Little Glass Slipper* by Marcia Brown, 1955

- *Madeline's Rescue* by Ludwig Bermelmans, 1954

- *The Biggest Bear* by Lynd Ward, 1953

- *Finders Keepers* by William Lipkind, illustrated by Nicolas Mordvinoff, 1952

- *The Egg Tree* by Katherine Milhous, 1951

- *Song of the Swallows* by Leo Politi, 1950

- *The Big Snow* by Berta and Elmer Hader, 1949

- *White Snow, Bright Snow* by Alvin Tresselt, illustrated by Roger Duvoisin, 1948

- *The Little Island* by Golden MacDonald, illustrated by Leonard Weisgard, 1947

- *The Rooster Crows* by Maude and Miska Petersham, 1946

- *Prayer for a Child* by Rachel Field, illustrated by Elizabeth Orton Jones, 1945

- *Many Moons* by James Thruber, illustrated by Louis Slobodkin, 1944

- *The Little House* by Virginia Lee Burton, 1943

- *Make Way For Ducklings* by Robert McCloskey, 1942

- *They Were Strong and Good* by Robert Lawson, 1941

- *Abraham Lincoln* by Ingri and Edgar Parin d'Aulaire, 1940

- *Mei Li* by Thomas Handforth, 1939

- *Animals of the Bible: A Picture Book* by Helen Dean Fish, illustrated by Dorothy P. Lathrop, 1938

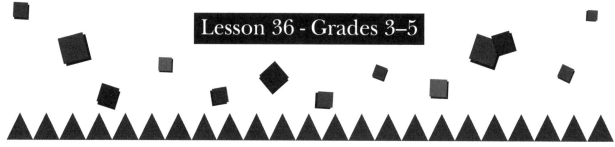

The Newbery Medal

Lesson 36 - Grades 3–5

Objective

Students will learn about the Newbery Medal.

Materials

- Newbery Bingo handout (page 136)
- Newbery Titles list (pages 137–139)
- Bingo pieces (buttons, small squares of paper, etc.)
- Prizes (optional)

Pre-Lesson Preparation

- Make several copies of the Newbery Titles list for students to share. Students will refer to the list when writing titles on their Newbery Bingo handout.

- Make a copy of the Newbery Bingo handout for each student.

- Make one copy of the Newbery Titles list and cut into strips. Place strips in envelope.

Lesson Procedure

1. Tell students that there is a special award given each year to the author who has made the most distinguished contribution to American children's literature in the preceding year. It is called the Newbery Award. Explain the following facts about the award:

   - The award is named after John Newbery. He was an English publisher and seller of children's books.

   - The award is given to encourage original, creative work for children.

   - The first award was given in 1922 to Hendrik W. Van Loon for his book, <u>Story of Mankind</u>. The most recent award was given last year to (provide name of author and title).

   - Some books win "second" place, a "Newbery Honor," for their outstanding contributions, too.

2. Students will become familiar with some of the Newbery titles by participating in Newbery Bingo.

3. Distribute a Newbery Bingo handout to each student. Distribute the Newbery Titles list to every few students to share. Students should refer to the list as they write one title per square on their bingo boards.

4. Draw a title strip from your envelope and read it aloud. If students have that title on their board, direct them to cover the square with a Bingo piece. The first student to complete a row horizontally, vertically, or diagonally, wins.

5. (Optional) Give a prize, such as a bookmark, to the winning student.

6. Play again as time allows.

Extension

Ask your students which books *they* would give the Newbery Award. Why? What makes that book special?

Allow students to make up an award to give to their favorite book.

Newbery Bingo

Place the book title of a Newbery Award winner in each square.

Newbery Titles

- *The Graveyard Book* by Neil Gaiman, 2009
- *Good Masters! Sweet Ladies! Voices From A Medieval Village* by Laura Amy Schlitz, 2008
- *The Higher Power of Lucky* by Susan Patron, 2007
- *Criss Cross* by Lynn Rae Perkins, 2006
- *Kira-Kira* by Cynthia Kadohata, 2005
- *The Tale of Despereaux: Being the Story of a Mouse, A Princess, Some Soup and a Spool of Thread* by Kate Dicamillo, 2004
- *Crispin: The Cross Of Lead* by Avi, 2003
- *A Single Shard* by Linda Sue Park, 2002
- *A Year Down Yonder* by Richard Peck, 2001
- *Bud, Not Buddy* by Christopher Paul Curtis, 2000
- *Holes* by Louis Sachar by 1999
- *Out of the Dust* by Karen Hesse, 1998
- *The View from Saturday* by E,L, Konigsburg, 1997
- *The Midwife's Apprentice* by Karen Cushman, 1996
- *Walk Two Moons* by Sharon Creech, 1995
- *The Giver* by Lois Lowry, 1994
- *Missing May* by Cynthia Rylant, 1993
- *Shiloh* by Phyllis R, Naylor, 1992
- *Maniac Magee* by Jerry Spinelli, 1991
- *Number the Stars* by Lois Lowry, 1990
- *Joyful Noise: Poems for Two Voices* by Paul Fleischman, 1989
- *Lincoln: A Photobiogrpahy* by Russell Freedman, 1988
- *The Whipping Boy* by Sid Fleishman, 1987
- *Sarah, Plain and Tall* by Patricia MacLachlan, 1986
- *The Hero and the Crown* by Robin McKinley, 1985
- *Dear Mr. Henshaw* by Beverly Cleary, 1984

- *Dicey's Song* by Cynthia Voight, 1983
- *A Visit to William Blake's Inn: Poems for Innocent and Experienced Travelers* by Nancy Willard, 1982
- *Jacob Have I Loved* by Katherine Paterson, 1981
- *A Gathering of Days: A New England Girl's Journal, 1830–32* by Joan W, Blos, 1980
- *The Westing Game* by Ellen Raskin, 1979
- *Bridge to Terabithia* by Katherine Paterson, 1978
- *Roll of Thunder, Hear My Cry* by Mildred D, Taylor, 1977
- *The Grey King* by Susan Cooper, 1976
- *M.C. Higgins the Great* by Virginia Hamilton, 1975
- *The Slave Dancer* by Paula Fox, 1974
- *Julie of the Wolves* by Jean Craighead George, 1973
- *Mrs. Frisby and the Rats of NIMH* by Robert C. O'Brien, 1972
- *Summer of the Swans* by Betsy Byars, 1971
- *Sounder* by William H. Armstrong, 1970
- *The High King* by Lloyd Alexander, 1969
- *From the Mixed-Up Files of Mrs. Basil E. Frankweiler* by E.L. Konigsburg, 1968
- *Up a Road Slowy* by Irene Hunt, 1967
- *I, Juan de Pareja* by Elizabeth Borton de Trevino, 1966
- *Shadow of a Bull* by Maia Wojciechowska, 1965
- *It's Like This, Cat* by Emily Neville, 1964
- *A Wrinkle in Time* by Madeleine L'Engle, 1963
- *The Bronze Bow* by Elizabeth George Speare, 1962
- *Island of the Blue Dolphins* by Scott O'Dell, 1961
- *Onion John* by Joseph Krumgold, 1960
- *The Witch of Blackbird Pond* by Elizabeth George Speare, 1959
- *Rifles for Watie* by Harold Keith, 1958
- *Miracles on Maple Hill* by Virginia Sorenson, 1957
- *Carry On, Mr. Bowditch* by Jean Lee Latham, 1956
- *The Wheel on the School* by Meindert DeJong, 1955
- *. . . And Now Miguel* by Joseph Krumgold, 1954
- *Secret of the Andes* by Ann Nolan Clark, 1953

- *Ginger Pye* by Eleanor Estes, 1952
- *Amos Fortune, Free Man* by Elizabeth Yates, 1951
- *The Door in the Wall* by Marguerite de Angeli, 1950
- *King of the Wind* by Marguerite Henry, 1949
- *The Twenty-One Balloons* by William Pene du Bois, 1948
- *Miss Hickory* by Carolyn Sherwin Bailey, 1947
- *Strawberry Girl* by Lois Lenski, 1946
- *Rabbit Hill* by Robert Lawson, 1945
- *Johnny Tremain* by Esther Forbes, 1944
- *Adam of the Road* by Elizabeth Janet Gray, 1943
- *The Matchlock Gun* by Walter Dumaux Edmonds, 1942
- *Call It Courage* by Armstrong Sperry, 1941
- *Daniel Boone* by James Daugherty, 1940
- *Thimble Summer* by Elizabeth Enright, 1939
- *The White Stag* by Kate Seredy, 1939
- *Roller Skates* by Ruth Sawyer, 1937
- *Caddie Woodlawn* by Carol Ryrie Brink, 1936
- *Dobry* by Monica Shannon, 1935
- *Invincible Louisa: The Story of the Author of* Little Women by Cornelia Meigs, 1934
- *Young Fu of The Upper Yangtze* by Elizabeth Foreman Lewis, 1933
- *Waterless Mountain* by Laura Adams Armer, 1932
- *The Cat Who Went to Heaven* by Elizabeth Coatsworth, 1931
- *Hitty, Her First Hundred Years* by Rachel Lyman Field, 1930
- *Trumpeter of Krakow* by Eric P. Kelly, 1929
- *Gay-Neck* by Dhan Gopal Mukerji, 1928
- *Smoky, the Cowhorse* by Will James, 1927
- *Shen of the Sea* by Arthur Bowie Chrisman, 1926
- *Tales from Silver Lands* by Charles Joseph Finger, 1925
- *The Dark Frigate* by Charles Boardman Hawes, 1924
- *The Voyages of Doctor Dolittle* by Hugh Lofting, 1923
- *The Story of Mankind* by Willem Van Loon Hendrik, 1922

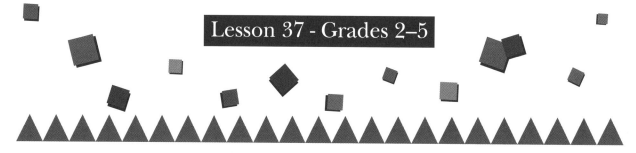

Guide Word World

Lesson 37 - Grades 2–5

Objective

Students will learn how to use guide words.

Materials

- Learning about Guide Words example (page 142)
- Guide Word World Game (page 143; includes board, pieces, and numbers)
- Dictionary Words game cards (page 144)
- Guide Word handouts (Practice 1, 2, and 3; pages 145–147)

Pre-Lesson Preparation

- Make a copy of the Guide Word World game board, game pieces and numbers for each group of 2–4 students. Cut out the board and laminate. Cut apart the game pieces and numbers and laminate.

- Make a copy of the Dictionary Words game cards for each group. Cut apart and laminate.

- Make a copy of the Learning about Guide Words Dictionary Example for each student, or display on document camera or overhead projector.

- Make a copy of the Guide Word practice handouts (1–3) for each student.

Lesson Procedure

1. Tell students that today, they are going to learn how to use guide words.

2. Explain that guide words are found at the top of the page of many reference resources including the dictionary, the encyclopedia, and the thesaurus.

3. Tell students that the guide words help us to locate words in these reference resources.

4. Distribute or display the Learning about Guide Words Dictionary Example as you discuss the following:

   - There are two guide words at the top of the each page.

   - The guide word found on the top left corner tells you the first word, or entry, on the page.

- The guide word found on the right top corner tells you the last word, or entry, on the page.

- You will find words alphabetically by using these two words as a "guide." For example, if you were looking for the word "ice," the guide words "hold" and "important" would tell you are on the correct page, because "ice" comes alphabetically between them.

5. Distribute the Guide Word World game board, game pieces, number cards, and a set of Dictionary Words game cards to each group of 2–4 students. Instruct students to follow these directions for the activity:

- Shuffle the Dictionary Words cards and place the deck face-down.

- Direct students to choose a game piece (book, paper, pencil, crayon) and place their pieces at "Start."

- Mix up the number cards 1,2,3,1,2,3 and place them face-down.

- The first player will draw from the Dictionary Words deck. If the word they draw falls alphabetically between the guide words "hold" and "important," then the student may turn over one of the number cards and move the designated number of spaces. Turn the number face-down again and mix. If the student draws a Dictionary Word that does not fall between "hold" and "important," then the student remains on his or her spot on the game board and the turn passes to the next player. Play continues until the first student reaches the "Finish" square.

Extension

For additional practice, direct students to complete the three Guide Words hand-outs (pages 145–147). These additional worksheets allow students to practice locating words by alphabetizing to the first, second, and third letter of a word.

Learning about Guide Words
Dictionary Example

hold

hold: to keep

huddle: to stand close together

hygiene: health

ice: frozen water

important

idle: lazy

igloo: Inuit home

ill: sick

important: significant

Guide Word World Game

 | | | 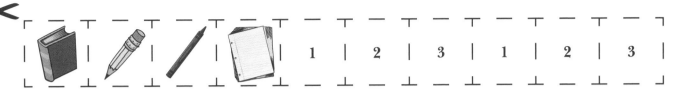 | | 1 | 2 | 3 | 1 | 2 | 3 |

HOLD

Start				
			Finish	

Dictionary Words

huddle	idle	igloo	hygiene	hive
ill	ice	him	history	help
humor	hum	hut	if	idea
ink	insect	into	itch	illegal
ignore	illness	item	ivy	in

Guide Words-Practice 1

A B C D E F G H I J K L M N O P Q R S T U V W X Y Z

Guide words are words that are found at the top of the pages in a dictionary, encyclopedia, or thesaurus. They help us to find words we are looking for.

Circle the eight words in the list below that you would find alphabetically between guide words "Eat" and "Nap." Use the first letter of each word to help you alphabetize. One has been circled for you.

EAT   NAP

FAN	PINK	APE	MOW
ICE	KIT	WORK	CAP
BUG	(LOG)	PET	RACE
HOT	DUCK	GONE	JAM

Now, put the circled words in alphabetical order.

1. _____   5. _____

2. _____   6. _____

3. _____   7. _____

4. _____   8. _____

Guide Words-Practice 2

A B C D E F G H I J K L M N O P Q R S T U V W X Y Z

Guide words are words that are found at the top of the pages in a dictionary, encyclopedia, or thesaurus. They help us to find words we are looking for.

Circle the eight words in the list below that you would find alphabetically between guide words "Effort" and "Etch." Use the first letter of each word to help you alphabetize. One has been circled for you.

EFFORT   ETCH

EVEN	ECHO	EDGE	EUROPE
EBB	EJECT	EYE	ERASE
EQUAL	(EGG)	ELBOW	EXACT
EMAIL	EIGHT	EACH	END

Now, put the circled words in alphabetical order.

1. _____   5. _____

2. _____   6. _____

3. _____   7. _____

4. _____   8. _____

Guide Words-Practice 3

A B C D E F G H I J K L M N O P Q R S T U V W X Y Z

Guide words are words that are found at the top of the pages in a dictionary, encyclopedia, or thesaurus. They help us to find words we are looking for.

Circle the eight words in the list below that you would find alphabetically between guide words "Dog" and "Doubt." Use the first letter of each word to help you alphabetize. One has been circled for you.

DOG   DOUBT

DOILY	DOWN	DOME	DONE
DODGE	DOT	DOLL	DOCTOR
DOZE	(DOSE)	DOE	DOPE
DOODLE	DOBERMAN	DOFF	DOVE

Now, put the circled words in alphabetical order.

1. _____   5. _____

2. _____   6. _____

3. _____   7. _____

4. _____   8. _____

Learning about the Dictionary

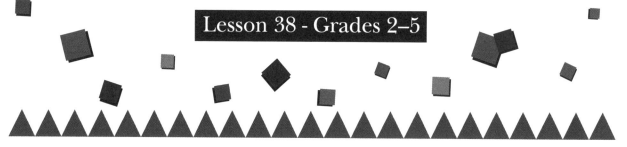

Lesson 38 - Grades 2–5

Objective

Students will learn how to use the dictionary.

Materials

- All about the Dictionary example (page 150)
- Using the Dictionary handout (page 151)

Pre-Lesson Preparation

- Make a copy of the Using the Dictionary handout for each student.
- Make one copy of the All about the Dictionary example.

Lesson Procedure

1. Tell students that today, they are going to learn how to use the dictionary.

2. Show the All about the Dictionary example to students on an overhead projector or document camera as you discuss the following facts:

   - A dictionary is a special book that contains a list of words.

   - All of the words in the list are in ABC, or alphabetical, order.

   - A dictionary tells us how to spell the words.

   - A dictionary shows how to pronounce the words.

   - A dictionary shows what part of speech the words are.

   - A dictionary tells us the meaning of the words.

   - Sometimes there is more than one meaning for a word. The first meaning is the one that is used the most.

   - A dictionary has two guide words at the top of the page to help us find the word we are looking for. The guide word at the top left corner tells us the first word, or entry, on the page, and the guide word at the top right corner tells us the last word found on the page. You can find words alphabetically by using these words as a "guide."

3. Have students practice their dictionary skills by distributing the Using the Dictionary handout for them to complete.

4. Discuss the answers.

Extension

Host a "Dictionary Champ" competition. Select two students to come to the front of the class. Give each student a dictionary. Call out a word. The first to find the word is the current Dictionary Champ. Choose another volunteer to compete against the reigning champ. Continue as time allows.

All about the Dictionary

- A dictionary is a special book that contains a list of words.

- All of the words in the list are in ABC, or alphabetical, order.

- A dictionary tells us how to spell the words.

- A dictionary shows how to pronounce the words.

- A dictionary shows what part of speech the words are.

- A dictionary tells us the meaning of the words.

- Sometimes there is more than one meaning for a word. The first meaning is the one that is used the most.

- A dictionary can show how many syllables a word has.

- A dictionary has two guide words at the top of the page to help us find the word we are looking for. The guide word at the top left corner tells us the first word, or entry, on the page, and the guide word at the top right corner tells us the last word found on the page. You can find words alphabetically by using these words as a "guide."

hide   hit

hide (hid) verb 1 : to not be seen 2 : the skin of an animal

high (hi) adjective : a position far above the ground

hill (hil) noun : a large mound of dirt

hire (hir) verb : to give a person a job

hint (hint) noun : a clue to the right answer

hip (hip) noun : joint of the body just below the waist

hit (hit) verb : a hard touch

Using the Dictionary

fold   fowl

fold (fold) verb 1 : to bend something over on itself

for•est (forest) noun : a large area with trees

fol•low (falo) verb : to come after something

for•give (fergiv) verb : to stop being mad at someone

foot (fut) noun : the body part below the ankle

foot•ball (futbol) noun : game played with a large, oval ball

four (for) noun : one more than three

fowl (faul) noun 1 : bird 2 : rooster or hen

Using the above dictionary page, answer the questions below:

1. What are the two guide words? _____ _____

2. What is the correct spelling for the word that means "a large area with trees?"
   _____

3. What is the correct pronunciation for the word "forgive"? _____

4. What part of speech is the word "football"? _____

5. What is the most used meaning of the word "fowl"? _____

6. Would the word "fox" be found on this page? _____

7. Would the word "foal" be found on this page? _____

8. How many syllables does the word "football" have? _____

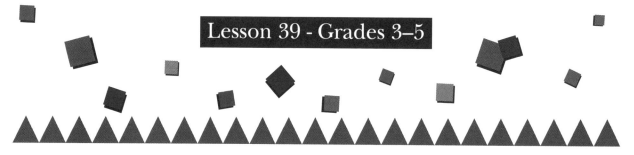

What's the Word

Lesson 39 - Grades 3–5

Objective

Students will practice finding words in the dictionary.

Materials

- What's the Word? handout (page 153)
- Dictionary Words (page 154)
- Dictionaries

Pre-Lesson Preparation

- Make several copies of the What's the Word? handout. Cut into strips.
- Make a copy of the Dictionary Words page. Cut the words apart.

Lesson Procedure

1. Tell students that today, they will practice finding words in the dictionary.

2. Distribute a What's the Word? strip to each student, as well as a word from the Dictionary Words page.

3. Direct students not to tell anyone the word they received.

4. Distribute dictionaries and allow students to complete the What's the Word strip for their dictionary words.

5. Choose four students to stand in front of the class. Have the students whisper to you which words they looked up.

6. Say one of the words aloud and have each student take turns reading their definition. Allow the class 2–3 guesses to identify the correct definition. Tell the student with the correct definition to step forward. Choose another student from the class to take his/her place.

7. Continue as time allows.

Extension

*During the What's the Word? activity, the class can be divided into groups and given points for selecting the right answer. Each group may only give one answer for the correct definition.

What's the Word?

What's the Word?

Name _____

Word _____

Definition _____

_____

_____ .

What's the Word?

Name _____

Word _____

Definition _____

_____

_____ .

What's the Word?

Name _____

Word _____

Definition _____

_____

_____ .

What's the Word?

Name _____

Word _____

Definition _____

_____

_____ .

Dictionary Words

mordant	industrious	laceration	garnish
quaint	quarry	rigor	roe
hoist	simper	stigma	teasel
jargon	kink	loiter	transom
trawl	urbane	vapor	vapid
audacity	bibliophile	confute	discord

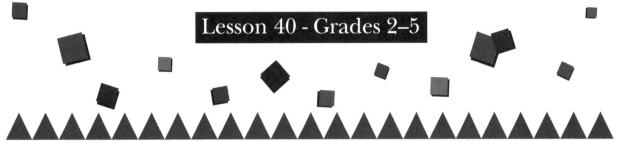

Learning about the Encyclopedia

Lesson 40 - Grades 2–5

Objective

Students will learn how to use the encyclopedia.

Materials

- Select a volume of the encyclopedia to use as an example during the lesson.
- Choosing an Encyclopedia handout (page 157)

Pre-Lesson Preparation

- Make a copy of the Choosing an Encyclopedia handout for each student.

Lesson Procedure

1. Tell students that today, they are going to learn how to use the encyclopedia.

2. Refer to your example volume as you tell students the following facts about encyclopedias:

   - Encyclopedias contain information about people, places, events, and things.

   - Each encyclopedia book is called a volume.

   - There are many volumes in a set of encyclopedias.

   - The volumes are arranged in alphabetical order from A to Z.

   - The volumes are also numbered.

   - The subjects in an encyclopedia are arranged in alphabetical order.

   - To find a subject, choose the volume that contains the first letter of the subject. For example, choose the Volume C when looking for information about cats.

   - Sometimes a subject contains two words, such as "New York." When that happens, look at the first word to find the subject. For New York, you would choose Volume N for "New."

- When looking up a person, choose the first letter of the person's last name. For example, choose Volume F when looking for information about Benjamin Franklin.

- If a person has a title, ignore the title and choose the first letter of the person's last name. For example, choose Volume R when looking for information about President Reagan.

- If part of the subject is abbreviated, spell out the abbreviation before looking it up. For example, St. Louis would be spelled out as "Saint" Louis in the encyclopedia.

- Tell students that the last volume in the encyclopedia is called an index. The index lists all of the subjects found in the encyclopedia, and the volume and page number where each subject can be found.

3. Tell students that they are going to practice selecting the correct encyclopedia volume for different subjects.

4. Distribute the Choosing an Encyclopedia handout to each student. Direct students to write the volume they would choose to find each subject on the handout.

5. Discuss the answers.

Extension

Have each student in the class write a subject on a piece of scrap paper. Collect the papers in a container. Divide the class into Team 1 and Team 2, and have the students sit on the floor in two parallel lines. Draw a subject from the container, and challenge the first player of Team 1 to identify the encyclopedia volume in which the subject would be found. If the player guesses correctly, Team 1 gets a point and play passes to Team 2. If the player guesses incorrectly, Team 2 has the opportunity to guess. Play continues until all subjects have been exhausted. The team with the most points at the end of the game wins.

Choosing an Encyclopedia

Write down the encyclopedia volume that you would choose to find the following subjects:

A	B	C CH	CI CZ	D	E	F	G	H	I	J K

L	M	N O	P	Q R	S SN	SO SZ	T	U V	WX YZ

1. Louis Armstrong _____

2. St. Helens _____

3. Tigers _____

4. Automobiles _____

5. France _____

6. New Year's Day _____

7. Helen Keller _____

8. Art _____

9. Football _____

10. Jazz _____

11. President Carter _____

12. Giraffes _____

13. Basketball _____

14. Music _____

15. St. Paul, MN _____

16. Dogs _____

17. Jupiter _____

18. Whales _____

19. Pelicans _____

20. Mars _____

What's the Word? Keywords

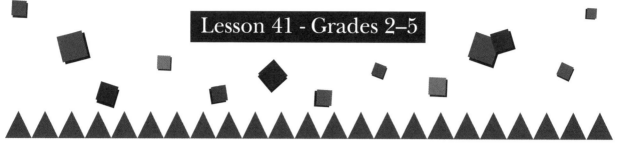

Lesson 41 - Grades 2–5

Objective

Students will review how to find information in a volume of the encyclopedia using keywords.

Materials

- Encyclopedia Scavenger Hunt handout (page 159)

Pre-Lesson Preparation

- Make a copy of the Encyclopedia Scavenger Hunt handout for each student.

Lesson Procedure

1. Explain to students that when they look up information in an encyclopedia, they must decide on a keyword to find the subject that they are looking for. The keyword is the best term to look up to help you answer the research question.

2. Distribute the Encyclopedia Scavenger Hunt handout to the class.

3. Direct the students to read the following rules silently as you read them aloud:

   - When looking for information about a subject, choose the first letter that the subject begins with. For example, choose C when looking up "Cats."

   - When looking for information about a person, it will be found under the person's last name. For example, the keyword for Abraham Lincoln would be "Lincoln."

   - When a subject contains two or more words, look up the first word. For example, New York would be found in the N volume for "New."

   - When a subject has an abbreviation, spell out the abbreviation when looking it up. For example, St. Patrick's Day would be found by looking up "Saint."

   - When a person has a title, look up the person's last name, not the title. For example, President Johnson would be found under "Johnson."

4. Review the scavenger hunt directions with students and have them complete the assignment.

5. If you choose, give students a prize, such as a bookmark, when they finish the hunt.

Encyclopedia Scavenger Hunt

Review the following rules for looking up a word in an encyclopedia:

- When looking for information about a subject, choose the first letter that the subject begins with. For example, choose C when looking up "Cats."

- When looking for information about a person, it will be found under the person's last name. For example, the keyword for Abraham Lincoln would be "Lincoln."

- When a subject contains two or more words, look up the first word. For example, New York would be found in the N volume for "New."

- When a subject has an abbreviation, spell out the abbreviation when looking it up. For example, St. Patrick's Day would be found by looking up "Saint."

- When a person has a title, look up the person's last name, not the title. For example, President Johnson would be found under "Johnson."

Circle the keyword in each question that will help you find the answer. Then, use the encyclopedia to complete the scavenger hunt questions.

1. What is the capital of South Dakota? _____

2. What is a meerkat? _____

3. What is one thing that Benjamin Franklin invented? _____

4. Where is Mt. Rushmore located? _____

5. Who is Sojourner Truth? _____

6. When was President Franklin Roosevelt born? _____

7. Where do wolverines live? _____

Encyclopedia Word Switch

Lesson 42 - Grades 2–5

Objective

Students will learn how volumes in the encyclopedia are organized, learn about finding information and notetaking, and practice crediting sources to avoid plagiarism.

Materials

- Encyclopedia Word Switch (page 162)
- My Subject Is . . . handout (page 163)

Pre-Lesson Preparation

- Make a copy of the Encyclopedia Word Switch subjects. Cut subject squares apart.
- Make a copy of the My Subject Is… handout for each student.

Lesson Procedure

1. Tell students that today, they are going to practice using an encyclopedia.

2. Tell students the following things to remember:

   - Each volume in the encyclopedia is arranged from A to Z, and each volume contains subjects that are arranaged from A to Z. For example, in Volume A, you will find "Ants" before "Apples."

   - There are guide words at the top of each page, just like in the dictionary, to help you find the word or subject you are seeking.

   - Each subject is called an "entry."

   - The information written about each entry is called an article.

   - When you are writing down information you find in the encyclopedia, don't copy it word for word. Instead, take notes. Just choose a few words (3–4) to help you remember the fact. Then, write it in your own words in your report. Copying someone else's work is called plagiarism, and it is against the law.

   - Always remember to write down where you got your information. This is called "citing the source." It gives credit to the person who wrote the material you are using. When you cite a source, write the author's name (found at end of article), the title of the article (usually in dark or bold print), the encyclopedia's name (found on the cover of the book), the city of publication (found on the title page), the publisher (found on the title page), and the copyright date (found on the copyright page or spine).

3. From the Encyclopedia Word Switch subjects that you cut out, distribute an animal subject to each student. Direct students to keep their words or subjects face-down.

4. Explain to students that they will be researching an animal in the encyclopedia today, but that they may not be researching the animal on the card in their hands. Tell students that first, they are going to play Encyclopedia Word Switch. Direct the first student to turn over his or her word and say it aloud to the class. Direct the next student to turn over his or her word. The second student may choose to keep his or her word, or "switch" it with the first student. The third student will then turn over his or her word and may keep it or switch with either the first or second student's words. Continue play until all students have revealed their words and had an opportunity to participate in the switch. At the end of the activity, students will research the animal they have at the end of the activity. Alternative: Cut out each animal subject and put in an envelope. Allow students to draw an animal to research.

5. Distribute the My Subject Is . . . handout to students and direct them to complete. Students can then turn their paper over and write a short paragraph about their animal subject using facts they learned in their research.

6. Remind students that finding information about a subject is called research, and that they must always write down where they got their information. Direct students to put this information at the bottom of the handout.

7. Have students present their research to their classmates.

Encyclopedia Word Switch

Anaconda	Black Widow	Chameleon	Condor	Coyote
Dingo	Electric Eel	Flying Fox Bat	Flying Lemurs	Giraffe
Horse	Iguana	Jellyfish	Jackdaw	Killer Whale
Komodo Dragon	Lion	Mudpuppy	Numbat	Ostrich
Python	Pelican	Quetzal	Rabbit	Sloth
Spider Monkey	Tiger	Toucan	Vulture	Wolverine
Yak	Zebra			

My Subject Is . . .

My Subject Is...

My subject is _____.

Three facts about my subject are: (Remember, don't copy the encyclopedia word for word. Just write a few words down to help you remember each fact.)

1. _____

2. _____

3. _____

Where I got my facts: (Cite the source.)

_____, _____. "_____."

   Author's Last Name   Author's First Name   Title of Article

_____. _____:

   Name of Encyclopedia Underlined   City of Publication

_____, _____.

     Publisher   Copyright Date

✄ —

My Subject Is...

My subject is _____.

Three facts about my subject are: (Remember, don't copy the encyclopedia word for word. Just write a few words down to help you remember each fact.)

1. _____

2. _____

3. _____

Where I got my facts: (Cite the source.)

_____, _____. "_____."

   Author's Last Name   Author's First Name   Title of Article

_____. _____:

   Name of Encyclopedia Underlined   City of Publication

_____, _____.

     Publisher   Copyright Date

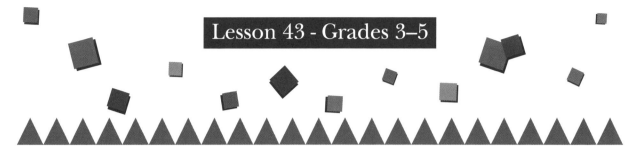

The Thesaurus Train

Lesson 43 - Grades 3–5

Objective

Students will learn how to use a thesaurus.

Materials

- The Thesaurus Is Helpful handout (page 166)
- Thesaurus Train Cards (pages 167–168)
- Thesaurus Train Cards Answer Key (bottom of page 165)

Pre-Lesson Preparation

- Make a copy of the Thesaurus Train Cards and laminate.
- Make a copy of The Thesaurus Is Helpful handout for each student, and one for the overhead projector or document camera.

Lesson Procedure

1. Tell students that today, they are going to learn about a book called the thesaurus.

2. Display The Thesaurus Is Helpful handout on a document camera or overhead projector as you explain the following facts:

   - A thesaurus is a book of synonyms.

   - Synonyms are words that have similar meanings.

   - A thesaurus helps you find words that make your writing more interesting and it helps you avoid using the same word over and over.

   - A thesaurus is arranged in alphabetical order.

   - A thesaurus has guide words to help you.

3. Allow students to practice using a thesaurus. Distribute The Thesaurus Is Helpful handout and direct students to complete. When they are finished, discuss answers as a class.

4. Students can continue to practice using a thesaurus and synonyms by participating in the Get on the Thesaurus Train activity.

Get on the Thesaurus Train

Distribute all of the Thesaurus Train Cards, even if that means some students will have two. Choose a student to begin by reading the question on his or her card. For example, "Who has a synonym for the word, 'happy'"? The student who has a synonym for the word "happy" will reply by stating the synonym on his/her card: joyful. This student then asks the question on his or her "joyful" card. The activity continues until all of the cards have been read.

Extension

Hold a "Thesaurus Champ" competition. Select two students to come to the front of the class. Give each a thesaurus. Call out a word with many synonyms, such as big, small, nice, etc. The first student to find the word is the Thesaurus Champ. Then ask the class who can give you a synonym for the word. Students should raise their hands to volunteer an answer. The Thesaurus Champ may call on his or her classmates. The first classmate to volunteer a synonym that is in the thesaurus for the word is the next student to play Thesaurus Champ. Continue as time allows.

Answers for the "Get on the Thesaurus Train" activity:

Happy–Joyful, Loud–Noisy, Pain–Suffer, Mad–Anger, Army–Troops, Ask–Request, Pretty–Beautiful, Hit–Pound, Fight–Brawl, Begin–Start, Mix–Stir, Brave–Courage, Concern–Worry, Baby–Infant, Cut–Split, House–Home, Rush–Hurry, Raise–Lift, Human–Mankind, Sick–Ill, Smart–Clever, Teach–Instruct, Rare–Uncommon, Living–Alive, Small–Little, Riches–Wealth, Most–Greatest, Friend–Pal, Stop–Halt, Frightened–Scared

The Thesaurus Is Helpful

lead

lead, guide

leader, guide, captain, master, director, chief, head

lean, tilt

learn, gain knowledge, master, find out

let up

least, smallest, slightest

leave, quit, abandon, depart

let, allow, permit

let up, pause, rest

Choose another word for these sentences:

1. The _____ told the people to listen.
   (leader)

2. The students will _____ important skills in school.
   (learn)

3. He would not _____ until he was finished.
   (let up)

4. He had to _____ his job.
   (leave)

5. Would you _____ her go on the roller coaster?
   (let)

Answer these questions:

1. What are synonyms? _____

2. How is the thesaurus organized? _____

3. How is a thesaurus useful? _____

Thesaurus Train Cards

SCARED

Who has a synonym for the word, "happy"?

JOYFUL

Who has a synonym for the word, "loud"?

NOISY

Who has a synonym for the word, "pain"?

SUFFER

Who has a synonym for the word, "mad"?

ANGER

Who has a synonym for the word, "army"?

TROOPS

Who has a synonym for the word, "ask"?

REQUEST

Who has a synonym for the word, "pretty"?

BEAUTIFUL

Who has a synonym for the word, "hit"?

POUND

Who has a synonym for the word, "fight"?

BRAWL

Who has a synonym for the word, "begin"?

START

Who has a synonym for the word, "mix"?

STIR

Who has a synonym for the word, "brave"?

COURAGE

Who has a synonym for the word, "concern"?

WORRY

Who has a synonym for the word, "baby"?

INFANT

Who has a synonym for the word, "cut"?

SPLIT

Who has a synonym for the word, "house"?

Thesaurus Train Cards

HOME
Who has a synonym for the word, "rush"?

HURRY
Who has a synonym for the word, "raise"?

LIFT
Who has a synonym for the word, "human"?

MANKIND
Who has a synonym for the word, "sick"?

ILL
Who has a synonym for the word, "smart"?

CLEVER
Who has a synonym for the word, "teach"?

INSTRUCT
Who has a synonym for the word, "rare"?

UNCOMMON
Who has a synonym for the word, "live"?

ALIVE
Who has a synonym for the word, "small"?

LITTLE
Who has a synonym for the word, "riches"?

WEALTH
Who has a synonym for the word, "most"?

GREATEST
Who has a synonym for the word, "pal"?

FRIEND
Who has a synonym for the word, "stop"?

HALT
Who has a synonym for the word, frightened"?

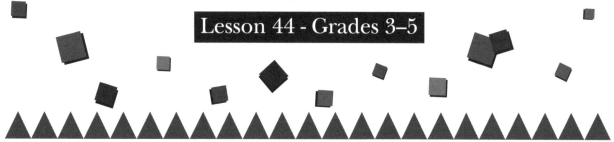

Cite the Source: Bibliographies

Lesson 44 - Grades 3–5

Objective

Students will understand how bibliographies are written and organized.

Materials

- Bibliography Examples handout (page 171)
- What's Wrong with the Bibliography? handout (page 172)
- What's Wrong with the Bibliography? Answer Sheet (page 173)
- Bibliography Practice handout (page 174)

Pre-Lesson Preparation

- Make a copy of the Bibliography Examples handout, the What's Wrong with the Bibliography? handout, and the Bibliography Practice handout for each student.
- Make one copy of the What's Wrong with the Bibliography? answer sheet

Lesson Procedure

1. Explain to students that after completing research, they must list the sources they used to get facts (books, encyclopedias, Web sites, etc.) at the end of the report. Explain that this list gives credit to the author(s) who wrote the source(s). The list is called a bibliography.

2. As you explain the following rules for putting materials in a bibliography, write them on the board:

   - Put the materials in alphabetical order by author's last name. If there is not an author, use the first important word in the title.

   - Be sure to include all of the punctuation marks.

   - Indent all of the lines except the first line.

3. Distribute the Bibliography Examples handout to each student in the class. Explain each of the examples.

4. Distribute the What's Wrong with the Bibliography? handout. Direct students to put a circle around anything that is incorrect in the bibliography. They can use their Bibliography Examples handout as a guide.

5. After each student has completed the assignment, discuss the answers.

6. Next, distribute the Bibliography Practice handout to each student. Direct students to choose a nonfiction book, encyclopedia, and Web site to practice writing bibliographies.

Bibliography Examples

Book

Author's Name (Last name, First name). <u>Title.</u> City of
    Publication: Publisher, Copyright Date.

Smith, Pat. <u>Rabbits: A Member of the Rodent Family.</u>
    Chicago: Leaf Press, 2006.

Encyclopedia

Author's Name (Last name, First name). "Title of Article."
    <u>Name of Encyclopedia.</u> City of Publication: Publisher,
    Copyright Date.

Hall, Jim. "Ants." <u>The World Book Encyclopedia.</u> Chicago:
    World Book Inc., 2005.

World Wide Web

Author's Name (Last name, First name). "Title of Article."
    <u>Title of Web site</u>. Date you got information (day Month
    year) <Web site>.

James, Bob. "Poetry For Kids." <u>Poetry4Us</u>. 12 May 2006
    <http://www.poetry4us.com>.

*MLA Works Cited Format

What's Wrong with the Bibliography?

In each example, circle the problem in the citation and correct it. You may use your Bibliography Examples sheet as a guide. When you are finished, number the citations below in ABC order as they would be found in a bibliography.

1. Sally Smith. <u>Pumpkin Time</u>. Chicago: River Press, 2005. *(See book example)*

2. McDonald, Fred. "Automobiles." The World Book Encyclopedia. Chicago: World Book, Inc., 2003. *(See encyclopedia example)*

3. Patterson, Jed. Lions in the Jungle. <u>Geography Alive</u>. 5 January 2007 <http://www.geographyalive.com>. *(See online example)*

4. Alden, Carrie. Baltimore: <u>Weather for the World</u>. Rocky Publishing, 2004. *(See book example)*

5. Peterson, Barry. "Dogs." <u>The World Book Encyclopedia</u>. Chicago: World Book Inc., 2007 *(See encyclopedia example)*

6. Duke, Ann. "Famous People." <u>U.S. Biographies</u>. 2 December 2006 http://www.usbiographies.com. *(See online example)*

What's Wrong with the Bibliography? Answer Sheet

In each example, circle the problem in the citation and correct it. You may use your Bibliography Examples sheet as a guide. When you are finished, number the citations below in ABC order as they would be found in a bibliography.

1. Sally Smith. <u>Pumpkin Time</u>. Chicago: River Press, 2005. *(See book example)*

    (Answer: Last name is not first.)

2. McDonald, Fred. "Automobiles." The World Book Encyclopedia. Chicago: World Book, Inc., 2003. *(See encyclopedia example)*

    (Answer: Encyclopedia is not underlined.)

3. Patterson, Jed. Lions in the Jungle. <u>Geography Alive</u>. 5 January 2007 <http://www.geographyalive.com>. *(See online example)*

    (Answer: Title doesn't have quotes.)

4. Alden, Carrie. Baltimore: <u>Weather for the World</u>. Rocky Publishing, 2004. *(See book example)*

    (Answer: Title and city of publication are reversed.)

5. Peterson, Barry. "Dogs." <u>The World Book Encyclopedia</u>. Chicago: World Book Inc., 2007 *(See encyclopedia example)*

    (Answer: no period at the end)

6. Duke, Ann. "Famous People." <u>U.S. Biographies</u>. 2 December 2006 http://www.usbiographies.com. *(See online eample)*

    (Answer: no brackets around Web site address)

Bibliography Practice

Bibliography for a Nonfiction Book

_____, _____. _____.
Author's Last Name   Author's First Name   Title of Article

_____: _____,
City of Publication   Publisher

_____.
Copyright Date

Bibliography for an Encyclopedia

_____, _____. " _____."
Author's Last Name   Author's First Name   Title of Article

_____. _____:
Name of Encyclopedia Underlined   City of Publication

_____, _____.
Publisher   Copyright Date

Bibliography for Web Site

_____, _____. " _____."
Author's Last Name   Author's First Name   Title of Article

_____. _____
Web site Title/Underlined   Date you got this information (day/month/year)

< _____ >.
Web site

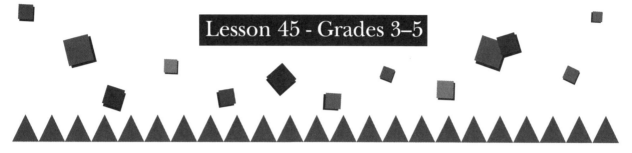

The Genre Results Are In . . .

Lesson 45 - Grades 3–5

Objective

Students will learn about different genres of literature.

Materials

- Genre Definitions handout (page 176)
- Several books depicting different genres
- Genre Survey (page 177)

Pre-Lesson Preparation

- Make a copy of the Genre Definitions handout.
- Cut into strips and paste each definition on construction paper.
- Laminate.
- Make a copy of the Genre Survey for each student.

Lesson Procedure

1. Explain to students that they will be learning about different genres of literature.
2. Tell students that "genre" is a French word that means "kinds."
3. Explain that a genre is a group of books that have certain things in common.
4. Choose a student to read the definition for each genre of literature.
5. As each genre is read, show an example of a book that corresponds to that genre.
6. Distribute a Genre Survey to each student. Direct them to put a check by their favorite genre to read. Collect the surveys.
7. Allow students to predict results. Share the results during the next class.

Extension

Make a bulletin board using the results from the survey. A bar graph can be utilized to show the results. Put questions on the bulletin board such as, "Which is the favorite genre to read?" or "Which is the next favorite genre to read?" Attach the definitions from the lesson plan to the bulletin board. In addition, put pictures of book covers on the board and ask students to identify which genre each cover belongs to.

Genre Definitions

Science Fiction: Made-up stories that mix technology and science. If you take the science out, there wouldn't be a story. Example: *Mrs. Frisby and the Rats of NIMH* by Robert C. O'Brien

Picture Books: Pictures are as important as the words in telling and understanding the story. Example: *The Snowy Day* by Ezra Jack Keats

Nonfiction: Gives information through true facts about a subject. Example: *Raccoons* by Lynn Stone

Historical Fiction: Mixes historical facts with realistic characters. Characters, language, and setting are from a certain period of history. Example: *Crispin* by Avi

Fantasy: Not real. Contains or is about something that could not have happened. Example: *Bunnicula* by James and Deborah Howe

Folktales: Stories that grow out of the lives and imaginations of everyday people through generations. Folktales are an attempt to explain and understand the natural and spiritual world. Example: *A Story, A Story* by Gail Hailey

Realistic Fiction: Stories that are made up but could happen to people or animals. Usually take place in the present. Example: *Frindle* by Andrew Clements

Poetry: Written in verse. Contains lines and stanzas and may contain rhyming words. Example: *Where the Sidewalk Ends* by Shel Silverstein

Biography: Story about a real person's life written by another person. Example: *Wilma Unlimited: How Wilma Rudolph Became the Fastest Woman* by Kathleen Krull

Genre Survey

Genre Survey
Boy___ Girl ____

(Pick Only One)

_____ Science Fiction

_____ Picture Books

_____ Nonfiction

_____ Historical Fiction

_____ Fantasy

_____ Folktales

_____ Realistic Fiction

_____ Poetry

_____ Biography

Genre Survey
Boy___ Girl ____

(Pick Only One)

_____ Science Fiction

_____ Picture Books

_____ Nonfiction

_____ Historical Fiction

_____ Fantasy

_____ Folktales

_____ Realistic Fiction

_____ Poetry

_____ Biography

Genre Survey
Boy___ Girl ____

(Pick Only One)

_____ Science Fiction

_____ Picture Books

_____ Nonfiction

_____ Historical Fiction

_____ Fantasy

_____ Folktales

_____ Realistic Fiction

_____ Poetry

_____ Biography

Genre Survey
Boy___ Girl ____

(Pick Only One)

_____ Science Fiction

_____ Picture Books

_____ Nonfiction

_____ Historical Fiction

_____ Fantasy

_____ Folktales

_____ Realistic Fiction

_____ Poetry

_____ Biography

Genre Bingo

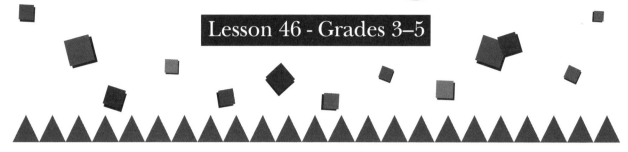

Lesson 46 - Grades 3–5

Objective

Students will identify books that correspond to different genres of literature.

Materials

- Genre Bingo handout (page 179)

- Prizes (optional)

Pre-Lesson Preparation

- Make a copy of the Genre Bingo handout for each student.

Lesson Procedure

1. Explain to students that they will be practicing putting titles of books into the correct genre.

2. Distribute the Genre Bingo handout.

3. Direct students to find a title of a book in the library that matches each genre listed on the handout. Tell them to write the title in the correct place on the handout.

4. To complete the task, all Bingo squares must have a title in them.

5. If you wish, reward students as they complete the task with a bookmark or other prize.

Genre Bingo

Historical Fiction	Realistic Fiction	Nonfiction
Poetry	Picture Book	Fantasy
Science Fiction	Biography	Folktales

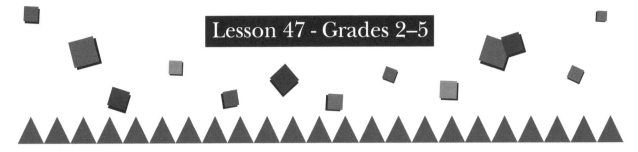

Media Maiden

Lesson 47 - Grades 2–5

Objective

Students will learn about the characteristics of fairy tales.

Materials

- One copy of the Media Maiden Cards (pages 182–184) per group of 4–6 students.

- Digital camera

- Printer

Pre-Lesson Preparation

- Using the digital camera, take a picture of the media coordinator, or another adult or student in the school. Print the photo out, and attach it to the Media Maiden Card.

- Make one copy of the Media Maiden Cards per group. Cut apart cards and affix to index cards. Laminate.

Lesson Procedure

1. Explain to students that they will be learning about the characteristics of fairy tales.

2. Show students the Media Maiden Cards. Tell students that there are facts about fairy tales on all of the cards except one card . . . the Media Maiden. Show students the Media Maiden Card. The goal of the activity is to avoid being the student who ends the activity with the Media Maiden.

3. Divide students into groups of 4–6. Choose one student to begin the activity. The student shuffles the cards and distributes them as evenly as possible to the other students. Students look at their cards and discard any pairs. The student who distributed the cards then offers his hand, face down, to the student on the left. The student randomly takes one card. If the card matches one he has, he discards the pair. If not, he keeps it. He then offers his hand, face down, to the student on the left. The activity continues clockwise until there are no more matches and the only remaining card is the Media Maiden.

4. After the activity, direct students to choose two of their pairs to read to the other students so that students can learn the characteristics of fairy tales.

5. Repeat as time allows.

Extension

The cards may also be used to learn about fairy tale characteristics by using them as a "Go Fish" activity or a "Matching" activity. Discard the Media Maiden Card when these activities are chosen.

Media Maiden Cards

Story ends with "They lived happily ever after."

Good character may live in a humble setting at the start of the story.

There are supernatural characters.

There is often a castle in the story.

There is often royalty in the story.

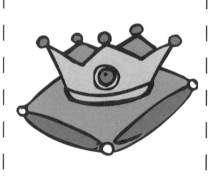

The good character versus the evil character.

Sometimes things happen in "sevens" such as "The Seven Dwarfs."

Good character meets magical helpers.

Media Maiden

There is magic in the story.

Evil character is punished.

Good character is rewarded with wealth.

Good character is rewarded with a happy marriage.

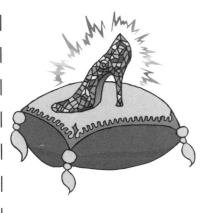

Things often happen in "threes" such as "three wishes."

There is a problem.

There is a solution.

Story begins with "Once Upon a Time . . . "

Story begins with "Long, long, ago . . . "

There is an evil character.

There is a good character.

Good character has bad luck.

Good character has to perform an impossible task.

Good character has conflict with an evil character.

Good character is not treated well.

Good character is in danger.

Folkworld

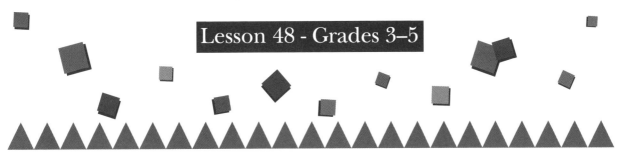

Lesson 48 - Grades 3–5

Objective

Students will learn the elements of folktales.

Materials

- Folkworld Game Board (page 186; includes board, pieces, and numbers)
- Folktale Characteristics Cards (pages 187–189)

Pre-Lesson Preparation

- Make a copy of the Folkworld Game Board for each group of 2–4 students and laminate. Cut apart the game pieces and numbers at the top of the page and laminate.
- Make a copy of the Folktale Characteristics Cards for each group to use with the game. Cut apart and laminate.

Lesson Procedure

1. Tell students that they are going to learn about the characteristics of folktales by playing a game called FolkWorld.

2. Distribute the Folkworld Game Board and a set of the Folktale Characteristics Cards to each group of 2–4 students. Direct students to follow these directions for the activity:

   - Place the Folkworld Characteristics Cards face-down.

   - Direct students to choose a game piece (book, paper, pencil, crayon) and place their piece at Start.

   - Turn the numbers 1,2,3,1,2,3 face-down and mix them up.

   - The first player draws a Folktale Characteristics Card and reads it aloud to the other group members. Then, the student will turn over one of the number cards and move the number of designated spaces. The number card is then returned, face-down, and mixed with the other number cards. Play passes to the next student. Continue until a student reaches the Finish square.

Extension

Discussion: Ask students to give examples of folktales they've heard. What are the tales about? What makes them folktales? Hold a storytelling session at the next class and, if they are comfortable, have students tell or read a folktale aloud.

Folkworld Game Board

| 1 | 2 | 3 | 1 | 2 | 3 |

Start				
				Finish

Folktale Characteristics Cards

Folktales are stories that grew out of the imaginations of everyday people, or "folk."

Folktales try to explain why or how things happen in the world (such as how the leopard got his spots).

Folktales started as oral or spoken stories.

In some folktales, animals and creatures talk just like humans do.

Folktales sometimes teach a lesson about how people should or should not act.

Folktales often start with "Once upon a time" or "Back in the days when animals could talk."

The setting of a folktale is usually a road, bridge, or forest.

Folktale stories have a problem and a solution.

At the end of the stories the "good" characters are rewarded and the "bad" characters are punished.

Folktales end with "and they all lived happily ever after."

In folktales, good behavior is rewarded and evil behavior is punished.

Folktales are usually short.

Folktale Characteristics Cards

Folktales have good characters and bad characters.

Folktales have been told for centuries, all over the world. Sometimes folktales try to explain certain customs and beliefs.

Folktales are fiction (not true) stories.

Trickster Tales, Fairy Tales, Myths, and Legends are all Folktales.

Folktales have been passed down from grownups to children for many years.

Some folktales are funny and make people laugh.

Folktales usually don't have a known author.

Most folktales are very old.

The action starts quickly in folktales.

Folktales are easy to understand.

A single folktale can have many oral and written versions.

People from different countries have their own favorite folktales.

Folktale Characteristics Cards

Folktales began as stories that were told to other people, not written down.

Examples of folktales are Jack and the Beanstalk, The Little Red Hen, and Anansi the Spider.

Don't pick a number. Quick! Go back two spaces and help Jack get down the Beanstalk.

Don't pick a number. Hurry! Go back three spaces and help the Little Red Hen bake her bread.

Don't pick a number. Quick! Go back one space and help the Three Billy Goats Gruff get across the bridge.

Don't pick a number. Hurry! Go back two spaces and help the Three Little Pigs escape from the Big Bad Wolf.

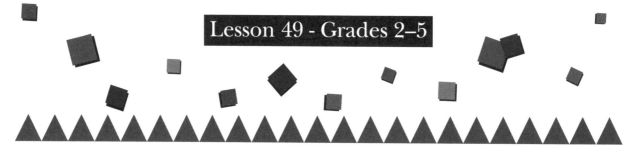

Take It or Leave It

Lesson 49 - Grades 2–5

Objective

Students will review library skills and terms that they have learned.

Materials

- Index cards

- Eight manilla folders with a pocket inside each (You can make a pocket by taping a 3x5 index card horizontally inside the folder. Tape all sides of the index card except the top.)

- Set of 7 Genre Terms and 1 Unrelated Term, Set of 7 Parts of a Book Terms and 1 Unrelated Term, Set of 7 Reference Terms and 1 Unrelated Term, Set of 7 Library Lingo Terms and 1 Unrelated Term, Set of 7 Dewey Decimal Numbers and 1 Unrelated Term (see pre-lesson preparation for details).

- Inexpensive prizes, such as stickers, bookmarks, erasers, pencils, pens, candy, discarded magazines, discarded books

Pre-Lesson Preparation

- Write the following sets of terms on individual index cards (one term per card), and include an unrelated term with each set. Paper clip related sets together with the unrelated term.

  Genre: Fantasy, Nonfiction, Biographies, Folktales, Historical Fiction, Realistic Fiction, Poetry, Mindy Mouse (unrelated term)

  Parts of a Book: Title, Author, Illustrator, Glossary, Index, Table of Contents, Copyright Page, Mindy Mouse (unrelated term)

  Reference Terms: Encyclopedia, Dictionary, Guide Words, Thesaurus, Bibliographies, Keywords, ABC (alphabetical) Order, Mindy Mouse (unrelated term)

  Library Lingo Terms: Caldecott Award, Newbery Award, Melvil Dewey, Folktales, Call Numbers, Fairy Tales, Author, Mindy Mouse (unrelated term)

  Dewey Decimal Numbers: 921 Biographies, 398.2 Folktales, 636.7 Dogs, 523.4 Planets, 743 Drawing, 796.32 Basketball, 551.5 Weather, Mindy Mouse (unrelated term)

Lesson Procedure

1. Tell students that today, they will be reviewing library skills and terms by playing Take It or Leave It, a game similar to the TV Show, Deal or No Deal.

2. Select a set of related cards. Place one card (including the unrelated term card) in each of the eight folders.

3. Choose eight students to stand in front of the class. Give one folder to each student.

4. Choose a student from the remaining class to be the first player on Take It or Leave It. This student should sit in front of the students who are holding the folders.

5. The player will choose a student to open their folder and read the index card inside it. If the student has a card that is a related term to the set, then the player can be offered a prize (sticker). If the player "takes" the prize, then the game stops. If the player "leaves"the prize (doesn't take it), then the player can choose another folder. If the player chooses a folder containing a related term again, he or she is offered another prize (bookmark). Again, the player may "Take It or Leave It." If at any point the player chooses a folder containing the unrelated term (Mindy Mouse), then the game is over. (*Note:* I usually offer the player a sticker as a "parting prize" if he or she chooses the unrelated term, just so no one walks away empty handed.)

6. Offer a series of prizes as the game progresses, with the most desirable prize at the end. You might even offer discarded books and magazines as prizes. A progression might be: Sticker, Bookmark, Eraser, Pencil, Pen, Candy, Magazine, Book.

7. Be sure to review each of the terms as they are revealed. For example, if the card says, "Historical Fiction," review what this means.

8. At the end of a game, collect the folders and replace the cards with a new set of related cards. Choose eight more students to hold the folders and another student to be the contestant.

9. Repeat as time allows.

Extension

You can make other sets of related cards. Remember to include one unrelated term with each set. Further topics might include Authors, Illustrators, Finding Books in the Library Terms, etc.

Library Jeopardy

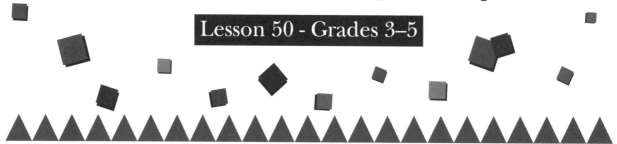

Lesson 50 - Grades 3–5

Objective

Students will review library skills/terms that they have learned.

Materials

- Jeopardy board
- Categories and answers cards
- Prizes

Pre-Lesson Preparation

- Make a Jeopardy board. Take a large piece of poster board and draw a 6x6 grid on it (six columns, six rows). Make the columns at least five inches wide, and the rows at least three inches high. Using 3x5 index cards, make a pocket in each box on the grid by taping three sides of the card and leaving the top open. You will have a total of 36 pockets.

- Write the following categories on separate index cards: Genre, Parts of a Book, Reference, Library Lingo, Finding Books in the Library, Media Miscellaneous. Place the category cards in the pockets at the top of each column.

- On individual index cards, write the answers (the questions in italics below) to the Jeopardy clues. Write the designated points for each answer on the back of each card. Arrange the answers in a column under the proper category heading from lowest point value to highest.

Genre Category

(10 points) True facts about a subject
(What is nonfiction?)

(20 points) A story about a real person's life written by someone else
(What is a biography?)

(30 points) Stories that are not real and are about something that could not have happened
(What is fantasy?)

(40 points)   Stories that are made up, but could happen to people or animals
(What is realistic fiction?)

(50 points)   Mixes historical facts with realistic characters
(What is historical fiction?)

Parts of a Book Category

(10 points)   The name of the book
(What is the title?)

(20 points)   Holds the book together
(What is the spine?)

(30 points)   Lists the chapters in the book
(What is the Table of Contents?)

(40 points)   Defines unfamiliar words in the book
(What is the Glossary?)

(50 points)   Lists all the subjects found in the book
(What is the Index?)

Reference Category

(10 points)   Definitions and pronunciations are found here.
(What is a Dictionary?)

(20 points) Set of books that contains information about people,
places, events, or things
(What are Encyclopedias?)

(30 points)   Contains synonyms for words
(What is a Thesaurus?)

(40 points)   The letter of the Encyclopedia you need to find information
about Thomas Jefferson

(What is J?)

(50 points)   The letter of the Encyclopedia you need to find information
about New Jersey
(What is N?)

Library Lingo Category

(10 points)   The person who does the pictures for the book
(Who is the illustrator?)

(20 points)   The best word to use when looking up information in
an Encyclopedia is called this.
(What is a keyword?)

(30 points)   Award given to the most distinguished contribution to American
              children's literature
              (What is the Newbery Award?)

(40 points)   These stories often end with, "And they all lived happily ever after."
              (What are Fairy Tales?)

(50 points)   List of resources found at the end of a report that tell where the
              report's information was found.
              (What is a Bibliography?)

Finding Books in the Library Category

(10 points)   What "Fic" means
              (What is Fiction?)

(20 points)   The book's address
              (What is a call number?)

(30 points)   Write the call number for a fiction book by Louis Sachar.
              (What is FIC/SAC?)

(40 points)   What the number 921 represents in nonfiction
              (What is biographies?)

(50 points)   How nonfiction is organized
              (What is the Dewey Decimal system?)

Media Miscellaneous Category

(10 points)   The person who wrote the book
              (Who is the author?)

(20 points)   Words written in verse
              May contain lines and stanzas that have rhyming words
              (What is Poetry?)

(30 points)   Award given to the year's best picture book
              (What is a Caldecott Award?)

(40 points)   The group of books that have the nonfiction
              call number 398.2: Folktales or Ships
              (What are Folktales?)

(50 points)   Name of the person who developed a way to organize nonfiction

              (Who is Melvil Dewey?)

Lesson Procedure

1. Tell students that today, they will be reviewing library skills and terms by playing Library Jeopardy! Put students into groups of 4–5.

2. Tell students that each group will select a category and a question for points. Students must give their answers in the form of a question. Provide a sample clue and answer. (For instance, "This is the color of the sky on a sunny day." Answer: *What is blue?*)

3. Select one group to go first. If the group answers its question correctly, it receives the designated number of points and it is the next group's turn. If the group answers incorrectly, then you may randomly select another group to answer the question. If that answer is correct, then the alternate group gets the points. If the answer is incorrect, then no points are awarded. Play continues with the next team.

4. When all questions have been answered, add up the points for each group. The group that has the greatest total points may choose a prize. Possible prizes include discarded magazines or books, stickers, pencils, erasers, candy, etc.

Extensions

- This activity is similar to the game "Password." Choose several review words from the Library Jeopardy game. (Words and phrases might include: call number, encyclopedia, author, title, genre, etc.) Select two students to start this activity. Whisper a review word to one of the students, and direct him or her to try to get the partner to guess the word by giving the partner clues. To make it challenging, give the team 15 seconds to complete the task. If successful, you might offer both of them a prize. For added fun, show the word to the whole class before the guessing begins.

- Create a Library Word Wall of all the terms learned during the year. Put the alphabet on a wall and under the apprepriate letter, place any new terms. Add to the wall as you discuss each term. A great way to visualize the year!

- Use the questions from the Library Jeopardy game to create a "Question Pot." Cut the questions into strips and place them in a container. Select a student to draw a question and try to answer it. If the answer is correct, reward the student with a prize (a sticker, choice of seat for the day, a discarded book, line leader, etc.). My students love the Question Pot and sit down quickly and quietly in hopes of getting picked for a turn. Usually, I do it at the beginning and end of class.